My Time With Einstein

My Time With Einstein

Stanley R. Cohen, Ed.D.

authorHOUSE®

AuthorHouse™
1663 Liberty Drive
Bloomington, IN 47403
www.authorhouse.com
Phone: 1-800-839-8640

Published by AuthorHouse   08/22/2012

ISBN: 978-1-4772-6263-4 (sc)
ISBN: 978-1-4772-6262-7 (hc)
ISBN: 978-1-4772-6261-0 (e)

Library of Congress Control Number: 2012915145

TABLE OF CONTENTS

Acknowledgments vii

Introduction ix

Chapter I: Getting started 1

Chapter II: The Science of Imagination 21

Chapter III: The Non-Scientific Side 29

Chapter IV: Albert and Nature 53

Chapter V: The Economist 59

Chapter VI: The Psychologist 69

Chapter VII: Einstein's Views on the Jewish Faith 75

Chapter VIII: The Future of the World 83

ACKNOWLEDGMENTS

My deep appreciation goes to Kathleen Hagen and Joan Cohen for their expert editing of the manuscript. Their feedback was critical in development of my story with Albert Einstein.

My heartfelt thanks to my wife, Joan, and to our five wonderful children, Steve, Ann, Donna, Claire, and Andrew. I love you all and forever. Your support through the years has inspired me to be the best human being I could strive to be.

INTRODUCTION

I met Albert Einstein in 1946 when I was a student at Rutgers University which was located about six miles from Princeton University where Einstein lived. I visited their library quite often, and it was there that I first saw him and introduced myself. For some reason, we had an immediate bond that lasted for about two years. I couldn't believe that a man of such importance would even speak to me, but he did. We had many one-on-one talks, and I learned about his theory of relativity as well his views on sociology, economics, psychology, education, and over-all philosophy of life.

This book describes many of those conversations that I can remember, but when I read about what some historians later said about him, I found many things that were different from what I knew. Those two years of my life were enriched by his presence. He became my hero, my mentor, and my inspiration to pursue my career with passion. He convinced me that making a contribution to other people was more important than money, so I pursued teaching, and after sixty years in the classroom, I have no regrets.

My friends, my family, my students and other professors at Nova Southeastern University of the Health Sciences have all encouraged me to write this manuscript because I am eighty-four years old, and they wanted the story written before my demise. I have complied because there is no one in history with a greater legacy for human rights than Albert Einstein.

experience. He made me realize that all of the so called experiments I had done in my own physics, chemistry and biology labs were not real experiments because the results were already known. He compared it to baking a cake from a cook book. A real experiment would have been changing the ingredients to see what would happen. Had I done this in my science classes, I would have failed the courses. Much of the literature about Einstein's life maintained he never failed traditional mathematics. However, you can only fail something to which you are exposed. He was introduced to the differential and integral formulas in calculus by reading a book, and his behavior at the Institute for Advanced Study clearly showed his mastery of these formulas. He often referred to the calculus as arithmetic, and he also learned algebra and geometry the same way. One afternoon he showed me his analysis of the Pythagorean theory and why it was true, but he refused the traditional logic leading to the formula. When I asked him about his love life, he saw himself as a failure in two marriages and a failure as a father to his two biological sons and one daughter. He really did not like to talk about his relationship with his wife or his children. However, one Friday afternoon he explained to me that both of his wives were constantly judging him, and he resented all the "should and should-nots" after sharing strong feelings he had for them. It was bad enough having the scientific world being critical of him as a person, but it was worse having this criticism coming from his family. His feelings were very strong, and he owned them, and he just wanted people close to him to understand without prejudice. He divorced his first wife, and he promised to give her the money he might get from winning the

Nobel Prize. He lived in Princeton with his second wife until he died. I was angered when I read another writer's perception that Einstein was a "ladies" man. I can assure the whole world this was not true, and I defy anyone to support that fact. I even asked him one day about the rumor, and he replied, "I wish that were true". However, that false idea may have come from his position that women should be allowed to attend Princeton University which at that time was for men only and from wealthy families at that. He wondered why women in this country were not valued as much as men and made lower salaries in positions of equal responsibilities. In the place of his birth, there were women doctors, dentists, engineers and scientists which he did not see in America. At that time, women in the United States were either guided toward teaching or nursing. In fact, the first female physician in the America graduated from Johns Hopkins in the early twenties. When she was admitted, Hopkins built her a separate bath room, and she had to study anatomy apart from the men.

I was fascinated by his concept that what was already known in science based on what could be observed represented a tiny amount of what really existed. He was certain that the realities of our universe existed even though they could not be observed. He was challenged many times concerning his objection to quantum mechanics because he believed reality should not be measured by concrete observation alone. He believed that faith in a concept was as good as actual observation. This puzzled me because his view seemed in conflict for his search for absolute certainty. Even his concept of God was based on his faith. He told me once that it did not matter if God really existed, but it was a necessary belief to explain predictable forces and patterns in the universe. He maintained that what he called soul energy was in every living thing. To him, the body was just a vehicle for that godly soul, and at the moment of death the body dies, but the soul returns to the global mass of all souls. He convinced me that if I nourished my soul with behavior that improved the lives of other people, my soul would grow and I would give back more than I got at birth. Although I never shared this with him, I had decided to become a teacher at that very moment because if I could improve the life of my students, my soul would grow even though money would be a struggle. I decided to accept his definition of soul energy because it meant something about me after death would live forever, a very comforting thought.

Einstein had some strong political beliefs. Because of his early exposure in Germany, he hated governments that dominated people. He really thought Adolph Hitler was a lunatic and prayed for his demise. He never spoke ill to me of any other people in the world. He believed that all human beings were basically born good and given a chance would be free of prejudice. He took issue with certain religious groups that were determined to convert everyone to their doctrine, and they would kill other people to achieve that goal. He was really aggravated when Senator McCarthy held his witch-hunt hearings in Washington D.C. that ended up destroying the lives of many people. I later found out that several of my best professors at Rutgers University were on McCarthy's list. They were unjustly labeled as communists and fired by the University. It took ten years for many of these people to get a job. He saw the university as the one place where all views could be examined without prejudice, and they should never become politically biased. When he was offered the job to become president of Israel, he said, "no" because he did not think he was capable of doing this. He told me that politics was more difficult than science. He said that nearly all politicians indoctrinate rather than educate the people to reach their own decisions. Indoctrination tells you what to believe. Education allows you to use your brain, think critically, and make your own judgments which may or may not agree with the political system. When I challenged him to think of ways to correct this, he said one word," democracy". "I would not want to live in a country that did not have civil liberty, tolerance, and equality for all." He also pointed out that this country is a great model for the rest of the world. People here own the government, not the reverse. He was also concerned that young people in this country may not appreciate what it is like to live without freedom of religion and freedom of the press. He loved the fact that people charged with a crime were considered innocent until proven guilty. In this way politicians cannot just charge opponents with a crime and put them in jail or even death to eliminate competition. This is what he experienced in Germany, and he was worried after the McCarthy hearings in the United States Senate that we were losing some of our freedom. I believe his rebellion against authority started at an early age because he felt helpless. No one in his early development thought he would amount to anything and often said so. He proved them wrong over and over again. Although it affected his self worth, he never stopped thinking and expressing his wonderful ideas.

Einstein had a different kind of brain. He could formulate pictures in his mind, and he learned best by doing this. For example, I found one idea in electronics that I knew, but he did not. It was how to generate an electrical frequency using an induction coil and a variable capacitor. I drew the following picture:

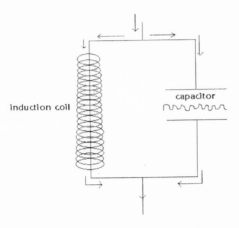

I explained the induction coil is just a coil of wire with a metal rod running through the middle. The capacitor is made of two pieces of metal separated by a dielectric with a rheostat. By placing these together in parallel, we can generate any radio frequency by simply changing either component. He was fascinated with this idea, and asked me to find him a bunch of parts to play with. He did not believe it was true until he confirmed it worked. He learned this idea when he looked at my drawing and imagined a picture of himself riding one side of the condenser, hitting a brick wall and unable to get to the other side. He literally became an electric current. I don't know how to label this unique way of learning. He could picture anything in his mind. What a rare talent.

The first time I saw the inside of his house I saw some interesting things. He had many compasses in just about every room. He also had a collection of different metals that he used to make his own compass. He figured out that only metals that had some iron or steel components would be attracted to the magnetic force of the earth. I also saw an abundance of watch parts on his desk. He loved to watch the gears turn and the effect large gears could have on smaller ones. He reminded me of my own childhood when I told my mother I loved watches, and she bought me a cigar box full of watch parts from a local jewelry in Washington, D.C. I played with those watches for several years and got to the point where I could repair and clean them. I used that skill to fix a grandfather clock that was stored in his house. He was very pleased I could do that. Frankly, I would have done anything to please him. He was my hero.

I also discovered in one closed room a bundle of unopened envelopes that were as old as five years. I opened several and found fairly large amounts of money. I believe many people thought he was poor and sent him checks. I made a large deposit for him, and I paid some of his bills. I tried many times to strike up a conversation with his wife, but with no success. I wanted to tell her how important Einstein was to develop scientific knowledge. She would simply leave the room. I never heard him tell her he loved her, and my impression was he tolerated her and nothing more.

The Institute for Advanced Study was built for Einstein to have a place to work. General Electric paid for the construction of the building and for all the expenses to run the place. It is located next to Princeton

University in New Jersey. They recruited 24 nuclear physicists who graduated from CCNY in New York where education was free if you were smart enough to pass their entrance exams. None of these men came from wealthy families, and they probably would never have gone to college unless it was free. I had never met a group like this. I could only describe them as brilliant. I am afraid because it cost so much to go to college today, thousands of students like these will be lost. Nothing is more important than the nurturing of young capable minds in order to save our society. I hope our politicians will listen to this and provide a way to subsidize education. Because of the GI Bill, a number of my family members returning from the war were able to go to college, and because they could achieve a college degree, they were able to support financially their own children to also get a college degree. Tax money to support education is well spent and may one day save our country.

I asked Einstein to share with me how activity at the Institute for Advanced Study produced the knowledge to make the atomic bomb. He explained at first they spent hours winding large electromagnets by hand because they were not available commercially. He explained that when an atom is bombarded by a neutron, it gives off energy and three more neutrons at specific angles. In order to get the chain reaction, the holes needed to be drilled precisely so each neutron would hit another particle. The other challenge was to get the speed of the neutrons up to the speed of light because Einstein said it was logical to do this. He was wrong about the speed and admitted that to me. The person who unlocked the mystery was Louise Meitner. She was working in a German lab where they had already cracked the atom.

Albert knew her from Germany, and he then wrote the famous letter to President Roosevelt to expedite the development of the bomb before the Germans got it. Hitler made a big mistake when he found out Meitner was Jewish and ordered her killed. She escaped and was brought to the Institute for Advanced Study. She told Albert there was a very narrow window with a short frequency range to get the reaction. Einstein and his co-workers had gone well above the correct frequency in their quest to get to the speed of light. This was all they needed, so the information was sent to the people at the Manhattan Project under army supervision where two bombs were constructed that were later used to level Hiroshima and Nagasaki. The Institute for Advanced Study was a unique place that probably never existed anywhere else in the world. They had a gigantic main-frame computer that occupied a large space. It was called the "Maniac" which stood for the "Mathematical and Numerical Integrator and Computer." Personal computers were not yet available. I believe that Freeman Dyson, a physicist at the Institute, was credited for its name. No engineering construction was done at the Institute. Every problem presented was attacked by theoretical mathematics. When no known differential calculus formula were appropriate, they wrote new ones. When these were later put to the test, they turned out to be correct. George Dyson, the son of Freeman, gave a beautiful description of the philosophy at the Institute in his book, "Turing's Cathedral." He said, "The Institute for Advanced Study had no laboratories, and was sort of the peak of the ivory tower. People were there to think great ideas, but not to build things, so mathematicians brought engineers into theoretical paradise against very strong objections. We don't want dirty engineers bringing wires and soldering guns and machine tools. Physically, they came into the building where all these great historians of classical art and so on were working, so there was great animosity." However by 1946, the year I met Albert, I did not see that kind of negative behavior especially after they saw the numerous outcomes shared by both groups. This was successful because of the great leadership of Albert Einstein. The mutual respect people had for each other, and the way they worked together was a great model for governments to behave. When someone spoke everyone listened. It was not who was sharing an idea, but the idea itself was the important thing.

One year after I met Einstein, Oppenheimer was hired to administer the program and several years later, he was declassified and blamed for leaking vital information. He believed that science belonged to the whole world. Actually what happened was that he sent information to Washington to be secured under army supervision, and the army by mistake put the data into a manual that was available to the whole world. They then blamed Oppenheimer and made him the scapegoat. In my view, Oppenheimer was a brilliant scientist, a great administrator and loyal to this country. He was not a traitor. The declassification was an awful blow to everyone at the Institute, and in particular, Oppenheimer who became extremely depressed. As far as I know he never received an apology for the charges that were made.

When Einstein received the Nobel prize in 1921, there are those who believe the award was for his theory of relativity. Actually that theory came much later in his work. The initial recognition was based on three papers he wrote prior to 1920. They were titled, "The Movement of Particles in a Liquid," "The Electrodynamics of Moving Bodies", and "The Proportion of Energy to Radiation". All of the concepts in these papers became the basis for his theory of relativity where he tried to explain that space and time were not absolute, but depended on the observer. So time and space always changed unless particles reached the speed of light which he maintained was absolute. A number of recent scientists have tried to prove that even the speed of light was not constant, but subsequent tests proved Einstein was right. When he published the three papers, many of the world physicists thought he was crazy because it came from an intuitive idea in his brain, and at that time, intuition was not considered a scientific basis for anything. It was only in 1924 when Jung published his book, "Personality Types", where he clearly defined a new respectable mental operation called "intuition" that the world of science really started to accept Einstein's gift of intuition. In fact the science world stopped making fun of Albert and considered him to be a genius.

While much of my knowledge came directly from conversation with Einstein, some of it I got from his book, "The World as I See it". It is a beautifully written piece of work, and I believe it deserves a place in the archives of the classics. In addition, he wrote five other books: "Ideas and Opinions". "The Evolution of Physics, "Relativity: The Special and the General Theory", "Out of my Later Years," and "Why Socialism?" All of these really describe his philosophy of life. He agonized over the atomic bomb being used in non-constructive ways.

Here are some of his quotes taken from his books, commentaries from other writers and from my personal experience with him:

"As long as I have any choice in the matter, I shall live in a country where civil liberty, tolerance, and equality of all citizens before the law prevail." He repeated this idea many times to me.

"The right to search for truth implies also a duty; one must not conceal any part of what one has recognized to be true."

"Imagination is more important than knowledge." Who else but a true intuitive would say this?

"If we knew what it was we were doing, it would not be called research, would it.?"

"The only reason for time is that everything doesn't happen at once."
"I don't believe in mathematics." Wow! What a statement coming from a superb mathematician.

"Science is a wonderful thing if one does not have to make a living at it." "Science without religion is lame, religion without science is blind."

"Do you believe in immortality? No, and one life is enough for me."

"Only a life lived for others is a life worth—while." This was his basic philosophy.

"So long as there are men there will be wars." He agonized over this idea.

"Nationalism is an infantile disease, the measles of the mind."

One of my favorites is: "Anyone who has never made a mistake has never tried anything new."

This quote from Einstein was adopted by the Alcohol Anonymous support group." Insanity: doing the same thing over and over again expecting different results." Isn't this what alcoholics do?

"I love to travel, but hate to arrive."

"The pioneers of a warless world are the youth who refuse military service." "The search for truth is more precious than its possession."

"Common sense is a collection of prejudices acquired by age eighteen."

"Common sense is not so common. It changes all the time."

"I never think of the future. It comes soon enough."

The statement that hit me the hardest and probably changed my life was, "What have you done to contribute to the world when you die? Are you just another breathing soul in the masses, or are you going to stand out and create a better world"? I have repeated these words in my mind for many years.

He also made some humorous statements like," Put on your pants before your shoes", "It's easier to throw out dishes than wash them." Intellectuals solve problems that would have been better to prevent." "Hair grows better when not cut, so why do it"? "Gravitation is not responsible for people falling in love," "The hardest thing in the world to understand is the income tax," "The most aggravating thing about the younger generation is that I no longer belong to it," and, "With fame I become more and more stupid, which is of course a very common phenomenon."

Perhaps his most unusual quote was "The compass was developed by a genius"

"The intuitive mind is a sacred gift and the rational mind is a faithful servant. We have created a society that honors the servant and has forgotten the gift" This idea is repeated many times in his writings.

"The relationship between energy, mass and speed of light should be obvious to everybody." Well it was not for me for a long time.

From his book, "The World As I See It", he explained his perception of man's purpose on earth, the meaning of personal happiness, and his passionate sense of social justice:

> "How strange is the lot of us mortals. Each of us are here for a short sojourn; for what purpose he knows not, though sometimes he senses it. But without deeper reflection one knows from daily life that one exists for other people—first of all for those upon whose smiles and well-being our own happiness is wholly dependent, and then for the many, unknown to us, to whose destines we are bound by the ties of sympathy. A hundred times every day I remind myself that my inner and outer life are based on the labors of other men, living and dead, and I must exert myself in order

to give in the same measure as I have received and am still receiving."

He goes on to explain why possessions one attains produce no real happiness:

"I have never looked upon ease and happiness as ends in themselves—this critical basis I call the ideal of pigsty. The ideals that have lighted my way, and time after time have given me new courage to face life cheerfully, have been Kindness, Beauty, and Truth. Without the sense of kinship with men of like mind, without the occupation with the objective world, the eternally unattainable in the field of art and scientific endeavors, life would have seemed empty to me. The true objects of human efforts—possessions, outward success, luxury—have always seemed to me to be contemptible."

He then describes his social and political views.

"My passionate sense of social justice and social responsibility has always contrasted oddly with my pronounced lack of need for direct contact with other human beings and human communities. I am truly a lone traveler and have never belonged to my country, my home, my friends, or even my immediate family, with my whole heart; in the face of all these ties, I have never lost a sense of distance and a need for solitude."

"My political ideal is democracy. Let every man be respected as an individual and no man idolized. It is an irony of fate that I myself have been the recipient of excessive admiration and reverence from my fellow-beings, through no fault and no merit of my own. The cause of this may well be the desire, unattainable for many, to understand the few ideas to which I have with my feeble powers attained through ceaseless struggle. I am quite aware that for any organization to reach its goal, one man must do the thinking and directing and generally bear the responsibility. But the led must not be coerced, they must be able to choose their leader. In my opinion the autocratic system of coercion soon degenerates; force attracts men of low morality. The really valuable thing in the pageant of human life seems to me not the political state, but the creative, sentient individual, the personality; it alone creates the noble and the sublime, while the herd as such remains dull in thought and dull in feeling."

He clearly explained his position on war:

"This topic brings me to that worst outcrop of herd life, the military system, which I abhor. This plague-spot of civilization ought to be abolished with all possible speed. Heroism on command, senseless violence, and all the loathsome nonsense that goes by the name of patriotism—how passionately I hate them!" He really considered military power a terrible threat to people everywhere.

A tribute to Albert Einstein:

Long after he died in 1955, a memorable was built in 1979 in Washington, D.C.at the Academy of Sciences. It took 22 years for the Academy to decide to do this. It is a twelve foot high statue, and at the top in large gigantic letters is the famous "$E=MC^2$" As I stood there, I wondered if most of the observers really understood the significance of his formula? It not only led to the atomic bomb, but also with his other theories led to thousands of things we have today in our modern world: from space flight to laser beams that might have taken another hundred years to develop were it not for this man. The time I spent with him I will cherish forever.

CHAPTER II

THE SCIENCE OF IMAGINATION

Albert Einstein loved to dream and use his imagination, even though he recognized that imagination was not really valued by most cultures. He also believed that children are born with the capacity to imagine the unknown until society makes them feel like misfits. He suffered as a child because his imagination at times was over the top, and he told me he hated school. He felt he was being smothered, so he tried to escape by playing hooky, pretending he was sick, and learning to play the violin. He loved to play classical music written by famous German composers. I saw him with tears in his eyes one day when playing certain music not out of sadness, but for pure joy. Whenever he could find a spare moment, he loved to go sailing and usually did that alone.

So why do I call this chapter the science of imagination? Where did scientific advancements like the light bulb, the concept of the wheel for transportation, nylon as a valuable clothing material, antibiotics for treating disease, radio and television waves, steri strips for closing wounds, stem cells for making new organs, refrigeration of food, computers, rockets, airplanes, and hundreds of others come from?

They came from people like Albert Einstein, Ben Franklin, Thomas Edison, Madam Currie, Selman Waxman and others who could think outside of the box by using their gift of imagination.

When I started working as a microbiologist, I soon discovered that the methods I had learned in my science preparation programs where not the way new things were discovered. I also developed a profound respect for the process of brain-storming because a group of five or six minds could generate hundreds of ideas in one hour. I was amazed that when others were expressing their thoughts, it generated ideas in me that I could not have done alone. While it was true that many of the ideas were not feasible, the few that were became extremely valuable and generated tons of money.

At the Institute for Advance Study located next to Princeton University in New Jersey, the primary method of discovery was brain storming for fresh ideas. Even after Einstein left, the Institute continued to invite scientists from all over the world who became visiting members and enjoyed a couple of weeks spent in creative thought. Among these were university professors who were not tied down with government grants either to write them or carry them out and were therefore free to use their imagination. Many of them said they were grateful for the experience and went back to work refreshed.

What can we do as a society to nourish the gift of imagination? As teachers we can acknowledge creative, intuitive behavior of all kinds. To simply tolerate such behavior implies we need to put up with what we label as misfits. This is not good enough. Children displaying creative thoughts and behavior need support and rewards of all kinds like positive teacher comments and positive grades. Teachers must move beyond simple labels of right and wrong to celebrate what is different and unique. We need to accept intuitive speculation which may even seem silly at times. Einstein loved fairy tales which he discovered as an adult. His mother never read them to him. In fact, because he could not pass the gymnasium test in Germany to go into fourth grade, his mother removed him from school and called him the "dummy" of her family. What an impact this had on his self esteem, and I believe he carried this with him for his entire life. Even though he received the Nobel Prize in 1921 for his work when he was only 42 years old, his self esteem was still very low in 1946 when I first met him. Would anyone ever believe that a man of such recognized distinction would have such a poor self image? Frankly, it made me very sad, but it taught me how important a mother's single sentence could impact on a person for a lifetime. My wife and I decided to always be positive with our five children even when small failures occurred as they were growing up. We tried to teach them that sometimes failure is really a good thing because the feedback shows us what we need to learn. I shared with them the story of Thomas Edison who had 10,000 failures in trying to find a filament for a light bulb before discovering tungsten. When asked why he did not give up, he said he learned what metals not to use. That's the positive use of failure. As scientists we need to teach children that single failures are only temporary and never final defeats. This is how we grow. This is how we raise the bar and achieve excellence. Our family motto became never, never, never give up. The difficult may take a little longer, but everything is possible. In Einstein's words, "Dream, dream, speculate, imagine and out of chaos comes truth".

Many have questioned Einstein's inability to go into fourth grade. He did not lack intelligence. He had a severe case of dyslexia, so he was a very slow reader because he had to reverse words in his mind. He also did not start talking until he was three years old. We now know that children who do not speak at an earlier age are not retarded, but both visual and auditory functions can be delayed and are really normal later in development. As an adult when I conversed with him in German, he spoke very slowly. That was an advantage for me because even after four years of German classes, I could not speak conversational German easily because I lacked the idiomatic expressions. He taught me his language.

He also taught me that all scientific laws were theories until they were proved right. This seemed to me to be a gigantic task because it suggested that every law I had learned in all of my sixteen years of schooling needed to be proven and re-evaluated. Also, he suggested that the only valid theories were those that improved the human race and led to a more efficient social world. I found that statement extremely interesting coming from a man of science. I began to realize exactly what he meant. He was against developing science that would lead to people destruction. He was against all war. He did not even believe we should have bombed Hiroshima and Nagasaki. Even though he was given credit for his work that led to the atomic bomb, he believed all nations should destroy these before we destroy the entire world. He was a gentle pacifist. The last thing he said to me was "How can we draft young men so they can fight wars, kill and be killed?" He thought politicians who would do this were a disgrace to mankind.

I was extremely fascinated with his personality. My first impression was he was very introverted, and he used his logical mind to analyze ideas as any great thinker would do. I was right about the introversion, but wrong about his thinking function. His introspection was powerful. He liked to work alone and he would think out loud. I once thought he was talking to himself, but it was his way of listening to himself. He also needed to understand a concept clearly until putting anything into action. He did not seek clear and objective rationale to learn something new. He did not like giving or receiving any critical analysis because he took these personally, and it hurt his feelings. He was very emotional and interested in other people's feelings. He wanted all the people in the world to get along in harmony. He never once reprimanded me for being late to pick him up. I believe his down to earth sensing function was quite low. He did not like to use standard ways to solve new problems. He liked using new skills rather than ones he already knew. He was unrealistic about how long it would take to solve simple problems because he would always get sidetracked and curious about other related ideas. He rarely reached a conclusion step by step and was impatient with details. New ideas inspired him more than what was known at the time, and he really trusted those inspirations if they were good or bad. His travel for several years was to take a train from Princeton to New York Grand Central Station. He had friends there who lived in the hotel directly above the station. One day I was told that he was running toward the gate while looking for the ticket in his pocket in order to get inside the appropriate gate, and after the conductor ushered him in, he said, "If I can't find my ticket, I don't know where I am going." He said this after taking this exact trip for several years, and he really meant it. So I decided that he was a strong introverted intuitive feeler, not an intuitive thinker as most writers have described him to be. Essentially he lived by his inspirations which made him so creative, and he had an imagination a mile wide. He did not see change as threatening, and he saw possibilities in everything. His world was chaotic, and he liked it that way. A look at his bedroom and his closets and his desk supported that conclusion. He insisted that order first starts with disorder. He was an intuitive genius, but at the same time he was a geographic moron. I told him that once, and he had a good laugh.

All the time I was analyzing his personality, I tried to get him to understand how concrete sensing people live in the present, and enjoy every moment of it now. If they miss the present and look around, it will be gone. The beauty of life for these people is not to dwell on the past or dream of the future. They don't worry about what has already happened or what may never happen. The importance of time is every minute of every day in the present. Einstein could not see how they could not enjoy life without speculating about the future. He wondered how a focus on time and worldly stuff for themselves could be real without compassion and empathy which he had as part of his feeling function.

In his own words he explained, "The most beautiful experience we can have is the mysterious. It is the fundamental emotion that stands at the cradle of true art and true science. Whoever does not know it and can no longer wonder, is as good as dead, and his eyes are dimmed It was the experience of mystery—even if mixed with fear—that engendered religion. A knowledge of the existence of something we cannot penetrate, our perceptions of the profoundest reason and the most radiant beauty, which only in most primitive forms are accessible to our minds. It is this knowledge and this emotion that constitute true religiosity. In this sense, and only this sense, I am a deeply a religious man. I am satisfied with the mystery of life's eternity and with a knowledge, a sense, of the marvelous structure of existence—as well as the humble attempt to understand even a tiny portion of the reason that manifests itself in nature".

Chapter III

THE NON-SCIENTIFIC SIDE

Although it took me a year of conversation with Einstein to understand his theory of relativity, I am convinced that most people do not and will not comprehend his reasoning because it was based on new mathematical and physical theoretical science. However, his views on education, politics, war, relationships, religion, wealth, freedom to explore, and philosophy are easy to understand. They are located in his book," The World as I See It." As a strong introvert, he became very assertive and aggressive when his emotions were roused, especially with human rights issues. Some authors describe him as an outgoing extrovert. I don't believe this was true because he always seemed to think out responses to my questions and slowly express his views. He was energized by his own internal brain, and he liked to work isolated in his quiet room. He did not like interruptions of thought, so I hesitated many times to bother him. He was best communicating on a one-to-one basis, and although he could function in a large group, it was not his preference. This may also have been based on his experience with large groups were he was ridiculed, laughed at, and called a lunatic. How many people could take that abuse and still pursue their dreams?

His situation was quite similar to that of the great German philosopher, Immanuel Kant, who introduced a new philosophical approach combining rational reasoning with human experience. Kant's early development began in poverty, and like Einstein he struggled to obtain an education. It took him many years to obtain the advanced degree so he could lecture at a university. At the university he wrote a number of papers applying his philosophy to science and mathematics, and I believe this is why he had so much influence on Albert. He liked him because he was so well-rounded as a poet, physicists, mathematician, and grounded in moral theology. Most philosophers before Kant were single minded like Descartes, Bacon, and Wolff. Einstein was very aware of their ideas, but he found them too limiting.

Einstein never had the money as a child or young adult to get an appropriate education, so he became an examiner at the Confederate Patent Office at Berne. This was a no brainer job, but it gave him a lot of free time to develop his theories of mathematics and physics. From patent office clerk came a job as a lecturer and then professor at a University. He eventually ended up as a professor of mathematics and theoretical physics at Princeton University where he stayed until his death.

His views on education mirror mine completely. He said," Academic chairs are many, but wise and noble teachers are few; lecture rooms are numerous and large, but the number of young people who genuinely thirst after truth and justice is small." Could it be that our thirst for money and social status has trumped the motivation to learn what is more important? Could it also be that the incentive to become physicians, lawyers, computer experts, and professional athletics far outweigh the incentive to become a great teacher. Teachers are the most important people in the world. They must mold people in every other profession, but today society undervalues their contribution. How many little Einsteins are crushed by insensitive teachers? What would it take to attract the kind of creative intuitive person to pursue teaching even if it meant living in poverty as did Einstein? I believe the values in society need to change and change drastically so that there is a clear safe environment for that special kind of learner to gravitate to become a teacher. In this particular time, our society values professional athletes more than their teachers. Einstein referred to this as, "the spirit of the times. "He argued that a hundred years ago university students had a respect for every honest opinion, the tolerance for which our classics had lived and fought." He also stated that "it was the students and the teachers at the universities who kept these ideals alive." It is even true today that professors and students at our great universities are still the only groups that can challenge power, politics, and money. If it ever happens that public education is gone, we are headed for disaster. However, in spite of such a threat, Einstein was still optimistic about the future. He used his humor to make fun of negative forces, and he suggested that without humor we would be paralyzed by reality. Many of his jokes were repeated over and over several times because he did not remember telling me. However, he never used profanity and described dirty comedians as a degrading force in our culture and especially to younger children who would accept them as good role models. He wanted young people to think about their purpose on earth and develop a social responsibility to help other human beings. Had he lived, he would have been thrilled with President Kennedy's famous inaugural declaration," Ask not what your country can do for you, ask what you can do for your country".

One thing you can do is to keep an open mind when politicians proclaim their views in a very passionate manner. Sometimes they have a hidden agenda which requires critical analysis. We need to judge issues based on our own knowledge obtained from books, not what others tell us to believe. A sound political society must be based on real truth, not the Madison Avenue public relations approach that can sell anything to anybody by cleverly planned manipulation. I understood what he meant because in my lifetime I saw how women would start smoking, drink beer, and go bowling all of which at one time were strictly limited to men. I remember when beer was sold in a large brown bottle, then in a smaller one with pink color along with an advertisement showing a beautiful wealthy lady surrounded by a large swimming pool. The statement on the picture was, "My best friends drink Peals." I also remember when cigarettes were made shorter, placed in a holder showing an affluent woman smoking. Even cigars which were originally brown and large, suddenly appeared shorter with a variety of colors appealing to women. When I was a youngster, bowling was a man's sport mostly in the cellars of buildings. They made it a family sport by building a large first floor facility with many having a play room for the children, so women could go bowling with built in sitters. Politicians with enough money can get votes using the same manipulation of ideas. When we look at the millions of dollars spent on political elections, it is easy to conclude that we can be sold a bill of goods no matter how bad the consequence might be. Adolph Hitler would have been a perfect client for Madison Avenue, but he didn't need them because he was a brilliant persuader of the non thinking masses.

Einstein has been labeled as a socialist, and I believe he was and was proud of it. That does not mean he liked socialistic governments. What he did like were social reforms which included social security, single electric and telephone companies, subsidies for farmers who provide our food, subsides for parks, roads, bridges, education, police and firemen. He explained in his book that our lives are really totally dependent on other human beings. He argued that our "Whole nature resembles that of the social animals. We eat food others grow, we live in houses others build, and we wear clothes others make." He believed that communication which is so important in the learning process was dependent on languages that other people created. Since his death we have research reports from several studies of people who have been raised in isolation for years, left alone and turn out to have primitive ideas and feelings. Yes, we are nurtured as individuals in a society of human beings with human values that influence us from birth to death. We judge the success of these individuals by how far their" feelings, thoughts, and actions are directed towards promoting the good of his fellows." The problem is if we accept was society has to offer now, we are stuck with limited resources. We need the contribution of creative thinkers to change and improve society or we will not improve. The concept is we can always do better. So the independent individual who is nurtured by society is also liberated to analyze and seek out better solutions, and new creative ideas so we don't become stagnant. In a sense there is never an end to this process. So when Einstein considered the health of society in his time, he saw a tremendous increase in world population, but a decline in what he called the great men. The achievements in art and music have not been great because they have lost their appeal to the masses. When he played his violin for me, he wondered if the old classical music would survive because it was not being valued and taught to young children. He thought we were robbing our children of one of the greatest pleasures of life. Yet he remained optimistic there would be a revival in the same way the classics in literature have survived the test of time. That optimism was also evident in his view of the future of the world. He did not agree with those who predicted an early end of civilization, and he said, "I believe better times are coming."

He based his conclusion on the concept that the rapid development of machines has decreased the amount of time individuals need to work to produce products, so the amount of their free time will gradually increase and they can focus on their own personal lives. He considered this a healthy change because in the early days of our national development most people spent 90 % of their time making a living using their hands to produce products. Machinery has made that process much more efficient.

In his writings, Einstein liked to make his points using stories about some of his close friends. For example, he paid tribute to Arnold Berliner who was an editor of a German scientific journal and who supported the notion that science and humanity can work together to make life better. The problem seems to be that as science becomes more and more specialized and narrowly focused, the "human intellect is and remains limited." He did not believe that most people were good at multi-tasking, so as science progressed, humanity could not keep up. Science investigators then become mechanics at best.

He loved Berliner because he insisted that journal articles in science were written in a manner that laymen could understand. It was not an easy task because many scientific specialists did not know the language of non-specialists. He also wrote the first physics book that contained basic principles that even the lowest of minds could comprehend. Einstein shared an interesting communication he got from Berliner. He asked me, "what is a scientific author?" and his answer was, "a cross between a mimosa and a porcupine." Many of his fights ended without success, but he did not give up which was a trait Einstein so admired. In his own words, "Berliner's fight for clarity and comprehensiveness of outlook has done a great deal to bring the problems, methods, and results of science home to many people's minds. The scientific life of our time is simply inconceivable without his paper. It is just as important to make knowledge live and to keep it alive as to solve problems."

Another of his close friends was a surgeon named Katzenstein whom he knew in Germany for eighteen years. During the summer months, he spent lots of time enjoying the professor's yacht and interacting with him sharing "experiences and emotions." which enriched his soul. Einstein found it very difficult to find people like him that would really listen and respond in a non-judgmental manner.

He considered his summer outings as therapeutic, and they made him fully alive. He wondered how a physician with so many responsibilities could find time to be a real friend in the face of phone calls relating to his duties such as patients who had just gone through high risk operations. He worried all the time about his patients because "they entrusted their lives to his care." Even so, he could separate that anxiety and still enjoy the beautiful lakes and forests of Brandenburg while he opened his heart to Einstein. I believe this is a case of one genius respecting another genius in a completely different field of work. What made his friend happy was finding ways to replace muscles, tendons, bones in such a way to "make patients fit for normal life." Many of his procedures were considered experimental, and he got much criticism from other physicians for trying new things. His accomplishments included successful treatment of ulcers without surgery and a cure for peritonitis using coli antibodies, not antibiotics. He had the same thirst for new ideas as did Einstein, but he also had the ability to implement these ideas when they turned out successfully.

In many places in his books, Einstein speaks about money in a very negative way because he observed how money became the prime motivator for setting lifetime goals. Money was used to buy what he called "stuff," all of which gives short term happiness. He told me if you work all day and get lots of money, but you do not get the satisfaction of making a contribution to another person, you will eventually get bored, hate your job, and hope for a quick retirement. I believe he was right. In my eighty-five years on earth I have seen so many people that fit that bill. For example, you are a mechanic building a new jet airplane. You work all day, and you are paid excellent salary. When you are working, do you think about why it is important to do this work carefully so that no crashes will occur, and people would get killed? Do you go home at night and just think about the money, or do you feel good because of your work that many lives will be safe? Yes, you get paid the same as any other worker doing the same job, but you have made a contribution far more rewarding to your soul. This idea is true in all professions, and I believe it makes the difference between loving your work and literally hating what you do.

Einstein's writings about religion, and his personal statements to me that I have referred to in this document are somewhat different. Keep in mind that he and his parents did not participate in traditional institutional practices. I do not see in his book his description of God as a massive collection of soul energy. I believed he changed his mind after I met him in 1946. His original writings, however, are worth consideration. He maintained that feelings and needs have led man to "religious thoughts" all of which are based on man's pure faith in the ideas and none of which can or should be proved by scientific evidence. The basis for primitive man's development of faith in religion was pure fear, "fear of hunger, wild beasts, sickness, and death." Lacking any real science, man can create beings for the purpose of protection in order to feel secure. He is suggesting here that God did not create man, but rather man created God. To get on the good side of God, man must behave in a manner consistent with the doctrine "handed down from generation to generation." He called this, "The religion of fear." To stabilize this process the role of priests, rabbis, and ministers was set up to be the "mediator between the people and the beings they feared." When religious leaders combine their roles with secular leaders, they develop common causes and become very powerful. Freedom of religion can be threatened by such a coalition, so the separation of church and state becomes paramount."

Einstein also maintained that another source for the development of religion were certain social forces which recognized that the general population were "mortal and fallible," and they needed "guidance, love, and support which came from a moral conception of God. The idea of God as the supreme being who "protects, rewards, and punishes" us, and loves us because we are his creation, and will preserve our souls after death, is a very comforting thought. He called this the "social or moral conception of God. He continued to argue the most of the world religions have adopted this definition of moral religion, all growing out of fear. He proposes that someday some individuals of "exceptional endowments" will generate a transformation of moral religion to "cosmic religious feelings" so that all people on earth will have a common bond to promote and help each other no matter their origin or where they live. I asked him to define his concept of God in such a religion, and he said it was a massive collection of soul energy but not limited to our earth, and when death occurs, individual souls never die, but are returned to God. He had strong beliefs in the separation of body and soul which I believe came from the Jewish scriptures. He had read the old testament several times as a child and as an adult, and while he rejected some of the institutional rituals he described as Pagan-like, he firmly believed in his idea of a higher power. Walking through the woods with him was a wonderful experience. He pointed out the order of many things in nature such as the stars, the bending of trees and plants, the sun and moon, the genetics of all living things that are predictable and probably not the result of pure chance. He saw in all of this an intelligence well beyond the capacity of man.

Another idea that disturbed Einstein was the battle between science and religion. Scientific thinkers are always basing conclusions on cause-effect of ideas. Because there is no way to prove the existence of God, how can any religious person say with any certainty that a God who rewards and punishes is a fact? However, Einstein argues "a man's ethical behavior should be based on sympathy, education, and social ties, so that no religious basis is necessary." He is saying that man can be good because it is the right thing to do. This idea threatens some clergy so they have "always fought science and persecuted its devotees." On the other hand, cosmic religious people are the greatest supporters to scientific research, and this support gives strength to scientists who are trying to understand the universe. He told me that man, alone, without higher power belief is too weak to endure the failures inherent in scientific research. He said this was a good idea even if not true.

Society expects scientific work to develop solutions to new concrete problems, and the money rewards depend on how good the results are. Einstein insisted that there be no practical ends in sight when goals are set. The pre-determination of research outcomes is too limiting. Open-ended studies may at some point find useful applications, but initially the purpose is "to blaze trails for industry." He declared "when scientific inquiry is stunted, the intellectual life of the nation dries up, which means the withering of many possibilities of future development." Through the years the main objections have come from the heads of governments who do not always like freedom of thought that may lead to political opposition. He cites the example of the Renaissance movement in Italy where the desire for truth was greater than all other desires, and the rise of civilization took huge leaps without political interference. All of this was accomplished by "the martyr's blood of pure and great men, for whose sake Italy is still loved and reverenced today."

Einstein did not believe that human liberty should ever be compromised by the State. He argued that "The pursuit of scientific truth, detached from the practical interests of everyday life, ought to be treated as sacred by every Government, and it is in the highest interests of all that honest servants of truth should be left in peace." He illustrates his concept with what he called, the "American patronage of science." He was so grateful to this country for accepting him personally as a representative of pure science without prejudice. He believed that material wealth and power have not been higher goals than the pursuit of science. I think he was being altruistic with this statement. I had many debates with him concerning the importance of power and material wealth in this country and around the world. It is my firm belief that most of the wars in the history of man have in some way originated from the "have-nots" wanting what the "haves" have. The struggle between the poor and the rich, the fights among different religious institutions, and the attacks by one country on another have had an economic base. I believe the Japanese attacked Pearl Harbor because we would not let them sell their products here, and although there were other factors involved, money was the primary root. I never won that argument with him, so we agreed to disagree. One thing for sure, he did not hate the Japanese as I did, and yet we both agreed on our feelings about the world onslaught of the Germans. However, to support his views about pure science goals, he cites the development of Davos University. This school was started by a group of people working together to try to prepare young people for a life enriched by a culture that was not supported by money and greed.

He said the University courses were a work of rescue being carried out to help young people who were troubled to use their intelligence to heal their emotional needs. He thought their sunny mountains helped cure some mental and physical problems that would allow them to exist. He also said, "they become a sort of hot-house plant and, when the body is cured, often find it difficult to get back to normal life." Yet, he believed intellectual work in addition to preparing them for a profession would also improve the hygiene of their minds. He insisted that the motivation to do this had to come from professors who could stimulate students and train their minds to be philosophers for intellectual lives.

Davos University was never dependent on any political purpose. Common feelings among nations were enhanced when there was an attempt to share in "some life-giving work." I remember an example he gave me. If the earth were suddenly invaded by outside forces, there would be a sudden cooperation among all nations to protect each other. All international conflicts would cease. The threat would be so great, that unless we acted together, we would be eliminated. Had Einstein lived longer, he would have been very disappointed to know that few Universities have been created that follow the Davos philosophy. It is still my belief that money and power have retarded that effort.

Another conflict I had with Einstein was concerning his view of George Bernard Shaw. He thought Shaw was independent and he could "see the weaknesses and follies of his contemporaries and remain themselves untouched by them." I agree that Shaw was a master at being critical of just about everybody, but I also think his criticism was not always constructive. It is good for us all to look in the mirror and asses truthfully what we do, but it is also true we need viable options to make changes that do not destroy our personal worth. For example, when Shaw made the famous statement, "those who can, do, those who can't teach," it really offended me. I loved most of my teachers, and I thought his criticism was destructive, unfair, and not helpful in improving education. Einstein was fascinated with Shaw's subtle humor, and thought he was extremely bright. I never questioned Shaw's intelligence, but his statements often resulted in people laughing at other people, not laughing with them, and they were deeply hurt. If he had ever looked at his own mirror, he would have seen how destructive some of his statements really were.

In a special speech Albert made, he said," You, Mr. Shaw, have succeeded in winning the affection and joyous admiration of the world while pursuing a path that has led many others to a martyr's crown. You have not merely preached moral sermons to your fellows; you have actually mocked at things which many of them held. sacred. You have done what only the born artist can do. From your magic box you have produced innumerable little figures which, while resembling human beings, are compact not of flesh ands blood, but of brains, wit, and charm. And yet in a way they are more human than we ourselves, and one almost forgets that they are creations not of Nature, but of Bernard Shaw. You make these charming little figures dance in a miniature world in front of which the Graces stand sentinel and permit no bitterness to enter. He who has looked into this little world sees our actual world in a new light; it's puppets insinuate themselves into real people, making them suddenly look quite different. By thus holding the mirror up to us all you have a liberating effect on us such as hardly any other of our contemporaries has done and have relieved life of something of its earth-bound heaviness. For this we are devoutly grateful to you, and to also fate, which along with grievous plagues has also given us the physician and liberator of our souls."

Albert saluted Shaw's methodology because he said, "He has delighted and educated us all." However, I saw him as a dogmatic one-sided heartless bitter old man without compassion or empathy. He only presented his ideas in one direction, never acknowledging both sides. That is not my idea of education. In order to have ammunition to debate this with Albert, I did some reading about Shaw's life. I discovered he was a socialist and wrote many speeches for the Fabian Society. That group was very angry about the exploitation of working class people, and Einstein certainly agreed with that idea. I also learned he was the only person ever to win both the Nobel Prize in Literature and an Oscar for his work on the film, "Pygmalion." I give him credit for some of those literary writings. However, I do not accept his lifelong hatred toward schools and teachers. He assumed because he saw schools as, "prisons and turnkeys in which children are kept to prevent them from disturbing their parents," as a valid argument against all schools and all teachers and all children and all formal education. It may have been true that for a minority of students the standard curricula were "useless, deadening to the spirit and stifling to the intellect." They certainly were to Albert, but to generalize this to the entire population of learners may get headlines, but is unsound thinking. I believe many children in America have benefited greatly not only for their intellectual development, but also for socialization reasons. After all, Shaw was educated in religious and other private schools where he did not mingle with the melting pot of students that attend American schools. He probably never saw a black child. His experiential background was very narrow and limited. I really admire Shaw as a play writer, but I cannot stomach his animosity toward all standard education. Albert and I agreed to disagree on this point. I really wish they were both alive so we could have more debate on the outcomes of American education.

When I examined Einstein's impression of America and other countries, I found some interesting views. He really thought we were outstanding in so many ways, but he acknowledged some of our important weaknesses as well. He saw our abundance of things like cars, washing machines, elaborate houses, beautiful clothing, air conditioners, and all the other materialistic things as a huge advantage over the standard of living in all other countries. He thought that knowledge and justice for all people was another great advantage, but the production of useful objects for daily living which were mostly accomplished by machines resulted in large loss of jobs. He cited in his writings that since labor was so cheap in countries like China and India because of overpopulation "we would probably not compete with them in the international market." Wow, was he right. Almost nothing today is made in America. Outsourcing has nearly wiped out our factories, and our politicians today are trying hard to restore those jobs. According to Albert, once our machines become super efficient, then and only then will our cost complete with cheap labor overseas. He admitted some questions do not always have rational answers.

As far as American people are concerned, Albert observed on his very first visit to this country that we have," a joyous, positive attitude to life." The smiles he saw of photographs were our greatest asset. Most Europeans see us as, "friendly, confident, and optimistic" since they come from environments which are more, "critical, self-conscious, and more pessimistic." He saw Americans as more ambitious, with an emphasis on the future. He also believed Americans were more consistent with their outlook on "moral and aesthetic ideas." He loved the idea that activities of the State in private lives is much more restricted than in Europe. I am not sure he would say this today because of the geometric explosion of government control over programs in finance, health care, education, and crime. Many of these benefit millions of people, but the organizations that are involved have had some serious issues with fraud. A good example might be the food stamp program for indigent people. Without it, many would starve and die, but the abuse has been significant. The principle is sound, but the administration is poor.

One negative view Albert had was while our beautiful buildings were a display of artistic talent, he thought that Europe was way ahead in the visual arts and music in the life of the people. He thought that art and music needed more emphasis and financial support in our public schools. I am in full agreement with this, but I also believe that adult classes in these fields would also improve our appreciation. He told me once that if private schools were ever supported by public funds, we would probably see the end of public education in America, and we would be headed toward education of the elite. It seems his prediction may come true. Private religious schools and private charter schools have been funded in recent years in many States. The money that could have been used to improve the public schools to make them better has been depleted. Religious people always had the right to send their children to their particular private school because they wanted them grounded in their own values, but they were also expected to pay for those institutions, not the government.

Albert had some strong views about other countries in the world. He was not an isolationist because he thought when problems exist in one country, it impacts on every other country including ours. He recognized American technical superiority, and he admired all the advances which were the result of our splendid research. However, he argued many times in his writings that, "Americans have not shown much interest in international politics." He insisted that we have a great responsibility not to be passive toward world problems because it would lead to disaster. A gigantic change has occurred since Albert's declaration of the necessity for world involvement. We have been the world's security protector with many countries, but at the same time we have paid the price with American lives and trillions of dollars in debt. We have borrowed huge sums of money from China that our children will inherit, and the ultimate goal he wanted was the end to wars and the disarmament of all nations. That has not happened. We have fought wars to end wars, and the result has been an escalation of countries to obtain more weapons. Sadly, I am becoming more of an isolationist. On the other hand, if we could figure out a way using intelligence to help other countries with food and medicine and education, I would be in favor of more debt. It is truly amazing to me that we have the smarts to go to the moon, but we can't seem to help other people with what they really need. We are always ready to budget money to fight wars, but it is always a battle to raise money for human needs. Of course, the lobby money from industry is designed to perpetuate wars because it keeps them in business so they make millions of dollars. A peaceful world would put them out of business. Here again is an example of how money and power can corrupt a society. Albert identified how," powerful industrial groups concerned with the manufacture of arms are doing their best in all countries to prevent the peaceful settlement of international disputes." He also suggested that unless the majority of people would support peaceful solutions, politicians would not act for fear of not being re-elected. In the history of our country, it appears we have had only a few statesmen, but lots of politicians. It is just not popular to be a pacifist. It is not popular to call for the end of all war. It is not popular to be a conscientious objector because you will be labeled a coward or even worse a traitor to our democracy. Government heads read the polls, and focus groups tell them what is not good politics. If democracy fails, it will be because the average person is not doing the kind of critical thinking that is really needed, so we have uninformed citizens voting. Albert told me our greatest hope are the young people in our country. Considering the tea party movement in 2010 which changed a lot of the politics in Washington, D.C, if we could get that kind of vigor and enthusiasm for the disarmament of nations, then new bills in our congress might be a real possibility. It will not be an easy sell.

He warns us with the following statement if we fail in this goal: "People seek to minimize the danger by limitation and restrictive rules for the conduct of war. But war is not like a parlor-game in which the players loyally stick to the rules. Where life and death are at stake, rules and obligations go by the board. Only the absolute repudiation of all war is of any use here. The creation of an international court of arbitration is not enough. There must be treaties guaranteeing that the decisions of this court shall be made effective by all the nations acting in concert, Without such a guarantee the nations will never have the courage to disarm seriously." He felt that there must be a limit to government sovereignty because of the fear and terror it brings without it. He argued the government "should be our servant and not we its slaves." He insisted that when governments force their people into military service, the "object is to kill people belonging to other countries or interfere with their freedom of development."

When I read his three page letter to Sigmund Freud, I found it hard to understand exactly what he wanted from Freud. I think he felt Freud was extremely well known all over the world, and he wanted his help to convince religious leaders to take up the cause for peace. I was not convinced that religious leaders were that sympathetic to Freud's work, and I saw no evidence of a response from Freud to Einstein. However, he insisted that war was a moral issue, and he expected religious leaders to support the moral rules found in the Ten Commandments. I don't think Albert realized the great threat to religious leaders that they might lose their congregation if they acted in a manner that did not agree with members of their group. When I was a doctoral student in education at Temple University in 1965, I met a theology graduate student whose dissertation was a result of a questionnaire he devised. He randomly selected one hundred religious leaders across all faiths from Maine to Florida, and one of his questions was, "Would you accept a black person into your congregation?" Not one of those surveyed said yes, and all hundred said they would lose their members. It made me realize that "love thy neighbor" only applied when it was convenient. However, I do believe that if that survey was done today, the results would be different. We have become much more tolerant in America. Albert would be proud.

Many of our conversations dealt with Albert as an active pacifist. He felt really bonded with the Flemish people after they had a huge peace demonstration. In the face of extreme criticism by public opinion, they stood their ground and fought for what they believed. The war machine makers lobbed their government to silence the demonstrators, but they did not succeed. However, the build-up of armaments continued, and the Flemish were not successful in getting other countries to join their effort. Einstein insisted that for pacifism to work, we need to try to "prevent the nations from arming," which will make them impotent to go to war. If all people would look at the history of wars, why they were fought, and what problems they solved, there would be no more killing. So many people still hold war as their ideal because military power gives them a feeling of superiority. They seem to compare countries like a battle on the football field where one team controls the game and wipes out all opponents. The difference is that wars end in numerous deaths on both sides, and no country really wins. If they believe they win, it is at the expense of the other side, so both lose. Albert thought the way to get pacifism started was to begin a movement encouraging young men and women to refuse being drafted. He called them the pioneers of a warless world and should be honored. The national media called them draft-dodgers and traitors. Even though he had very strong commitment to Israel, he opposed the law requiring every young person except the orthodox Jews to serve in the military. A political battle is still raging in Israel whether or not to continue to allow the orthodox to abstain from serving. In fact as our war fronts in America expand, and our military forces are depleted, there are those asking for a return to the draft. A wiser solution is to bring our troops home, and we need to figure out other ways to solve the multitude of problems that exist in the world which will really help in the long run. These methods require real mediation, real caring for other people besides ourselves, and a determination that peaceful solutions are good for all people in all countries. Einstein called this the "liberation of humanity," and he believed that the way to get acceptance from other countries was to send them what they really needed. Instead of guns and tanks, they need food, they need treatments for disease, they need hospitals, they need decent modern schools, and they need the modern conveniences of living like cars, washing machines, air conditioners, and supermarkets. According to Albert, Europeans see our standard of living as a dream come true. If we stop spending billions of dollars making wars, we might have the resources to help other nations achieve what we have.

CHAPTER IV

ALBERT AND NATURE

I had the opportunity to drive Einstein around in a Chevrolet through parts of New Jersey, and his comments on those trips convinced me he had a love affair with nature. In Germany he never saw cows being milked by machines, nor chicken farms where egg laying was mechanized. On one visit to a chicken farm in Lakewood, New Jersey, the farmer explained to him that chickens lay eggs only in the morning when the sun comes up. Einstein had an immediate response. "Why not trick the chicken and turn the light on in the middle of the night. They might lay eggs twice that way." Sure enough that idea caught on, and egg production sky-rocked across America. One thing he was trying to figure out for several months was why light energy stimulated chickens' natural cycle. On a subsequent visit to the farm, he asked if light also increased rooster desire to copulate with chickens. The farmer said "no" because roosters copulated any time anywhere a chicken was available all day long. Our next place to visit was a corn field in Hightstown New Jersey. He loved to eat corn on the cob, but when he saw cow manure spread across the corn field without first being sterilized, he lost his desire. The Borden Dairy farm was another place that fascinated him because second to water, milk was his primary drink. When he was a child, he drank milk from certified cows that was not pasteurized. He truly believed that the taste of American milk was different from what he drank in Germany. He asked me if I thought pasteurization was doing something to milk besides controlling bacteria, and if so, could that change be detrimental to digestion. At the time I really thought his question was over the top, but in recent years that question has been raised again by a number of medical scientists. I pointed out to him that children in Europe were being infected with tuberculosis by drinking contaminated milk, and the sacrifice in taste was worth doing to prevent disease.

When I took him to Rutgers University to meet Selman Waxman, the two bonded like they were brothers. He knew that Waxman discovered streptomycin which was the second known antibiotic after Fleming discovered penicillin in 1929. He also knew that Waxman donated the entire profit of one million dollars to Rutgers University which was used to build an entire new campus across the Raritan river. The result was a new chemistry research building, a new biology building, and a new football stadium. Waxman showed Einstein how he got five hundred soil samples from all over the world because he thought the soil in New Brunswick was dead, and the sample from Turkey contained the fungus from which he found streptomycin. Albert liked the fact that Waxman was so creative, and he saved the lives of thousands of people around the world. The notion that there were millions of organisms in the soil with each controlling the growth of the other was a revelation to Einstein. He wondered what was the nutritional source to feed all these things. He said if we could get the answer to that, we might be able to end the death of thousands of children dying from starvation all over the world. Because of his interest in soil, I gave him an inexpensive microscope I had in my room that I used to look at slides. I showed him how to make a slide, stain it with a dye and look for organisms. I supplied him with a half dozen cultures filled with nutrient agar and a special sterile needle to collect and grow bacteria. He became an excellent student of microbiology which did not surprise me because he was good at everything he did. I believe his curiosity was the motivating factor in his exposure to anything new.

Our next adventure was to the Swift meat packing facility where we watched all kinds of meat products being prepared for market. I remember asking him if he wanted to really know what was put in hot dogs, and he passed on this offer since he wanted to continue eating them. However, when he learned they were putting sodium nitrate in most all their packaged meats to keep the meat red, he really got angry. The reason they gave was when meats were kept in the super markets after a couple of days, they would turn brown, and no one would buy them. The Swift decision was made strictly on money, but Albert wanted to know why there were no labels indicating the use of chemicals that could be harmful to the body. We got no logical answer to that question.

Some of our travels were much more pleasant. A visit to Mount Pleasant, New Jersey in a local department store, he met up with a salesman that he knew as a child in Germany. It was the first time I ever saw Einstein hug another person. Hugging was just not his thing. In fact, he did not like other people touching him, nor did he like to shake hands. He was extremely careful about his hygiene, often washing his hands several times a day especially after he saw the microorganisms from the slides he made. I constantly reminded him that some bacteria like lactobacilli were good for people, and did not cause disease. They really do protect us in many ways from disease organisms. He was skeptical that this was true.

Because he was interested in art and animals, I had to cross the bridge into Philadelphia, and take him first to the Art Museum. He was not thrilled about climbing the huge steps, but when we got inside, I think he was hypnotized. There were several hundred paintings, and he wanted to see every one of them. I think we were there about four hours, because he did not want to leave. He was really overwhelmed with the art, so we decided to go to the zoo another day. On the way home he was telling me about the mental pictures he had of some of the art, and he even remembered the names of some of the painters. However, modern art paintings did not move him emotionally. He tried to analyze the meaning of such art, but he said it was beyond his comprehension. My come-back was always "nothing is beyond your cognition."

Several weeks later in 1947, we went to the Philadelphia Zoo. We went early in the morning so we would have enough time to see everything. He was like a kid in a candy store. He had never seen some of these animals, and he thought it was cruel to lock them up because he felt all living things should be free. As with people, animals have a right to liberty. He asked me how I would feel encaged liked these poor animals. My response was, "Isn't that what we do when we lock up criminals in jail?" Several of the writings at each animal cage surprised him. Giraffes sleep standing up because if they lie down, they can't get up. So they lie down only when they die. Each sign had the expected longevity for each animal, and they were all different. This affirmed the idea that there were lethal genes in each animal that kick in at the time of death. I had shared this with him after one of my required biology courses. If this were not true, then why do pet dogs who have the best love and care rarely live beyond fifteen years of age? When we passed the monkey facility, two of them were copulating, and he thought they should have some privacy. He offered to send the attending a screen for that purpose, but the response was not positive. He gave Albert a weird look. I don't believe he knew who he was. Anyway as we walked by the lions, even though we were separated by a moat filled with water, he was visibly frightened, and I asked him why. He believed that lions could swim and jump a much greater distance than across the moat especially when they are angry. So we moved quickly to the bird sanctuary where there were all kinds of beautiful birds. They were on both sides of the walk-through, and we stayed there for half an hour watching them, and Albert tried to talk to them even though they were behind glass barriers. He smiled at the birds, and told me their colors were just another form of light energy with a variety of frequencies. The talking parrots were especially interesting to him, and he was amazed at the sounds they could reproduce. There were a number of other trips we took in the Chevrolet, and the question might be raised why that car? Even though there were also other cars available such as Fords and Chryslers, the word "Chevy" was commonly referred to when one talked about cars. If you bought a car, you bought a Chevy. General Motors had a great public relations advantage just by the name. That lasted for many years, but after the second world war when foreign imports were coming into America, they lost their advantage. American car makers could not compete with cheap labor in other countries.

Chapter V

THE ECONOMIST

As far as I know, he had no formal education in the science of Economics, but his views were amazingly perceptive. Maybe his lack of access to all the economists of the world was a good thing because none of the famous people in this field agreed to anything. When I tried to share with him what I had learned in my economics class at Rutgers about Keynesian versus Neoclassical economics, he challenged both of these theories, and in fact, the debates still continue in our present day economy. Arguments about how our recession started or whether trickle-down economics really works or whether government subsidies to failing banks or industry can pull us out, still continue. I remember pointing out to him that the Keynes's concept when people start saving money and spend less, depressions are sure to happen. Albert really felt that the larger issue was the number of poor people who had so little money, and most of them could not even save any money. The result was over-production, under consumption, followed by more over-production and piling up of large inventories. This would make prices drop until they reached a level where poor people could buy products again. The demand driven economy only worked when people had enough money to purchase things.

In Einstein's writings he tried to distinguish between real and apparent over-production. He said, "By real over-production I mean a production so great that it exceeds the demand. This may perhaps apply to motor-cars and wheat in the United States at the present moment, although even that is doubtful. By over-production people usually mean a condition of things in which more of one particular article is produced than can, in existing circumstances, be sold, in spite of a shortage of consumption goods among consumers. This condition of things I call apparent over-production. In this case it is not the demand that is lacking but the consumers' purchasing power." In essence, he did not believe that overproduction was responsible for a crisis in the economy. He also believed that the tariffs we placed on foreign goods coming in would increase prices and decrease purchasing power. Although he never told me directly that we should lower taxes on the middle class and increase taxes on the wealthy, I believe he would have agreed that any government intervention with resulting increase in money for lower and middle class families would help strengthen our economy. Politicians who advocate this idea today are labeled socialist.

Albert also had some strong views concerning the responsibility of the German government to compensate surviving families of the six million Jews who were killed in Hitler's slaughter camps. He was quite disturbed that the United States was pouring money in to rebuild German cities, but at the same time was not pressing the Germans to pay for their crimes to the survivors. It was only when a large Jewish population sued the German government that reparations started. Many of the families who were lucky to escape or who were liberated from the camps at wars' end were quite ill and needed a whole lot of medical and psychological help. It has been estimated that as high as thirty percent of those migrating to this country suffered from Crones disease many of which needed expensive surgery. Crone was a surgeon in New York, and performed his surgical procedure on hundreds of immigrants even if they could not afford to pay. He was a great humanitarian.

When the Nuremberg trials took place, and the heads of the Nazi slaughter camps were called to task, I recall their defense was they were simply taking orders from higher-ups. The court ruled that their acts were immoral, and they were responsible for all the killings. Everyone charged was found guilty, but it took over fifty years to find them all because they were hiding all over the world. The same moral responsibility principle has been used to convict American soldiers who have committed atrocities in Viet Nam and the middle-east wars. I believe this was one of the reasons Einstein hated war. We place young men and women into battle for long periods of time in living conditions that promote anxiety and depression, and then we expect them to make sound moral judgments even when they are facing enemies who want to kill them.

At first glance, one might conclude that Einstein's pacifism was similar to other well known Americans like Henry Ford and Thomas Edison. This is completely false. I remember Albert showing me a clipping about a training camp in Sussex County, New Jersey where the American Nazi Bund party was training young men to join their rebellion against America for fighting the war in Germany. The prime money support according to Albert came from Henry Ford, one of the richest men in the United States. This was shocking news to me. I knew that Ford had a reputation as an anti-Semite, but I had no idea he was willing to put his money and reputation into an effort over many years to degrade American Jews. I decided recently before writing this story, I would check out the facts about Ford since it meant so much to Einstein. Everything he said was true. The American German Bund Party was establish in 1936, and its first mission was to prepare propaganda aimed at Jews who were boycotting businesses in Yorkville, a neighborhood in Manhattan with a large German population. There was strong evidence that the Bund had the same platform as that of Hitler's Nazi Party, and there was no question that Ford's money paid for everything. That included four round trip peace ships for hundreds of people to Europe, and expenses for training youth in Camp Nordland, Camp Siegfried in New York, Camp Hindenburg in Wisconsin, and Camp Bergwald in New Jersey. The Bund held numerous rallies the largest of which occurred on President's Day, 1939, in Madison Square Garden, New York. Nearly 25,000 sympathizers attended the rally. The president of the party was Fritz Kuhn, an American born German. It is on record that he referred to President Roosevelt as "Franklin Rosenfeld," and said he started the New Deal to please all the Jewish bankers. Nearly every rally ended with violence between protesters and Nazi Bund storm troopers. I can see now why Einstein was so worried about these meetings. I believe it reminded him of similar rallies in

Germany before he left the country. Also, he was very happy when a law suit was filed by our government against Ford, but some historians believe the suit was dropped because Ford made a public apology. When Ford's children took over the business, they tried very hard to establish a positive relationship with the American Jewish people. However, the public relations damage was so great that even today many Jews will not buy Ford automobiles.

Although he was pessimistic about controlling the economy in a capitalistic system as ours, he had some interesting ideas on how to solve the depression other than government spending on armaments. He believed that it was possible to have a planned economy but still maintain our capitalistic model in which consumption goods are produced and distributed by the community. "The necessary controls would have to come from individual free enterprise." However, Einstein had more faith in individual freedom to control production and consumption than I do. To me, the inherent element of a dog-eat-dog economy to survive leaves little room for one business to care about another. While a centralized system of government can stymie innovation, if properly managed, it can really keep price controls steady and avoid the peaks and valleys of a depression. It seems clear to me that when there are controls on maximum working hours and controls on minimum wages that can be adjusted from time to time, there would be a better chance of stability in the marketplace Opponents would call this position socialism, and they would cite the Russian model as an example of how that concept would fail. On the other hand, Einstein really thought it worked well in Germany He argued in his writings,

"In the development of human civilization, one must remember that culture in the highest forms is a delegate plant which depends on a complicated set of conditions and is wont to flourish only in a few places at any given time. For it to blossom there is needed a certain degree of prosperity, which enables a fraction of the population to work at things not directly necessary to the maintenance of life; secondly, a moral tradition of respect for cultural values and achievements, in virtue of which this class is provided with the means of living by the other classes, those who provide the immediate necessities of life".

He felt that Germany was a good example in the past hundred years where both conditions were evident. Prosperity while only modest was certainly sufficient and the "respect for culture was vigorous." In the latter part of the century, prosperity had declined because the industries had been cut off from sources of raw materials that nearly strangled them. So the surplus for the intellectual workers started to decline, and "a fruitful nursery of culture turned to wilderness." Beilstein which at one time was the elite science journal in all the world, was eventually put to rest and died. As a student in high school interested In becoming a scientist, in 1943, I was told I needed to take German to prepare me to read that famous science journal. By the time I graduated from college, the journal had lost its popularity.

Albert considered the demise of culture in Germany a tragedy initiated by Adolph Hitler to promote what he called "national egotism". He insisted that this is what can happen when community feeling is overpowered by a government who is interested only in wealth and power. From Albert's time until recent years, this is exactly what I believe has happened in America. Government money to support the cultural arts has declined to an all time low, and it probably won't come back soon. Political leaders in both parties tend to follow the will of the people, and right now, cultural concerns has taken a back seat.

In a letter written to Herr Cederstrom, Albert responded to his proposal to solve some of the world's economic problems. His statement about what to do with the very young and the very old was worth considering. For one thing he was in "favor of abolishing large cities, but not of settling people of a particular type—e.g. old people—in particular towns." He was horrified by the idea of an old people's isolated ghetto apart from all others. He also insisted that inflation would eat up the meager income that most of the elderly would get from social security. He really felt that the very young could benefit greatly from the elderly because in just living itself, a great deal of wisdom is accumulated from experience alone. He observed how the older people in our community were being put out to pasture with little consideration for their value. He declared, "What a waste in human resources." He reminded me that age was never a factor in recruiting scientists for the Institute for Advanced Study. He also remembered thinking when he became twenty-two how much smarter his parents were when he was eighteen. Einstein was a champion for all minorities one of which were the elderly. The other groups that concerned him were religion and the American people of color. He shared with me that when minority groups have distinguishing physical characteristics or even special names, they are automatically tagged as inferior. It seemed to him that most people always think that the majority are smarter, better—looking, and much more acceptable He believed that this is why minorities are treated unfairly and according to his writings suffer socially and economically. He said, "Under the suggestive influence of the majority, most of the victims themselves succumb to the same prejudice and regard their brethren as inferior beings. This second and greater part of the evil can be overcome by closer combination and by deliberate education of the minority, whose spiritual liberation can thus be accomplished." He further stated that "The efforts of the American negroes in this direction are deserving of all commendation and assistance." To me, he expressed a fascinating concept. The very people who suffer the greatest possible prejudice themselves, will in fact mirror that same behavior with other minority groups. Maybe this is why children who suffer from alcoholic parents tend to continue the same pattern because this is what they know to do. Sometimes individuals in the same minority will exhibit antagonistic behavior against others because of simple differences in physical appearance. A number of sociologists have observed the apparent prejudice of lighter skinned blacks against very dark blacks. I believe that Albert really thought that all prejudice was based on ignorance, and very often was the result of sub-conscious memory. I had a personal experience years ago when I was a public school administrator. I attended a conference of educators where we were shown pictures and credentials for four hours of prospective teachers looking for work. We were asked to rate these on a graded scale from 1 to 10. In the afternoon we were given a second set of pictures and credentials and asked to rate them for hiring. Actually the credentials were the same as the morning session, but half of the teachers were given a black face without our knowledge. There were several hundred administrators involved. Without exception, every teacher with a blackened face got lower scores from the group. I could not believe that I did this because I had always prided myself in never being prejudice. It had to be some kind of sub-conscious thing which I have never figured out, but it was true, and it made me feel ashamed.

I wonder if the majority/minority concept would apply to different political nations. Could it be that smaller less powerful nations are suffering from prejudice? The economic conditions in these countries is quite different from our own. We tend to like the affluent nations because they are more like us.

Isn't that the same behavior exhibited by all prejudiced groups. Do most of us really care about the four thousand children who die every day from starvation?

Chapter VI

~*~

THE PSYCHOLOGIST

Einstein was an avid reader of the works of many American psychologists. Much of the information came from the Presidential Addresses of the American Psychology Association. I saw some copies that dated back to 1894 when William James wrote," The Knowing of Things Together." He even knew about John Dewey who was one of my favorite psychologists and educators. It was Dewey who wrote the famous book, "Democracy and Education" which has become a classic for educators around the world. There were many things that Albert disagreed with. For example, Dewey argued that, "Students will remember little of what they hear, some of what they read, lots of what they see, but nearly all of what they understand." To Einstein, the understanding comes from internalizing what is intuitive, and everything else starts with that. However, he did agree that Dewey's idea, "You learn to do by doing" was probably correct except that doing what is incorrect results in misconceptions that soon become so solid that no change in knowledge is possible. I asked him what he thought of the idea "Tell me, I forget. Show me, I remember. Involve me, I understand." He said that if "involve me" meant active participation of a willing open minded brain, then learning will be enhanced. Otherwise the old adage, "You can take a horse to water, but you cannot make him drink" is probably very true especially for long term memory.

Albert also had a copy of Henry Marshall's, "The Methods of the Naturalist and Psychologist." He liked Marshall because he explained things with language that every human could understand. Even though Einstein respected Sigmund Freud and his reputation world wide, he really thought he was using terms like superego to explain important things, but the invention of new psychological terms made the whole concept impossible for the common man to understand. In fact Albert did not think many of Freud's ideas were even new at all. On the other hand, Carl Jung, a friend of Freud, wrote a beautiful book describing different personality types of normal people, and he accomplished this using ordinary language. He told me he was puzzled why noted respected scientists of the mind would use elite terms that only other professionals would comprehend. He cited examples like the work of Edward Thorndike and Robert Yerkes who were able to communicate their ideas with simple language. Yerkes paper on "The Psychology in Relation to War" was very important in shaping Albert's attack on all wars.

One problem area I observed about Einstein that I have not seen in the literature was his absolute addiction to pipe smoking. Keep in mind that in 1946 the great majority of university students and faculty smoked pipes. It was the thing to do. Nearly all actors in the movies were either smoking cigarettes, pipes, or cigars. I was also a victim until my brother sent me a colored picture of three men playing chess, smoking pipes, with huge cancerous lesions on their lips. I sent my pipes home with my laundry box, and I never smoked again. Even after I showed Albert the pictures, he could not stop nor did he want to. He told me he really enjoyed smoking because it relaxed him. He knew he was addicted and was very dependant on his pipe. I nagged him over and over to quit to no avail. I even told him how the smoke in his house was affecting my asthma. I learned a lot from this experience. All addictions are horrible because we lose our ability to make decisions that can extend our life free of disease. On the other hand, some addictions may in fact be really good for people. Einstein's love for sailing after he left the Technical Institute and his love for playing Mozart's music with his violin later in life, were all good addictions.

Since he was interested, I got him some material written by Clark Hull concerning adaptive behavior. He thought the ideas expressed in that writing could be used to change the pattern of thinking with individuals who become mass murderers and just kill other people because they are psychopaths. This past year we have two such events in Colorado that killed innocent people, and in both cases the shooters got a thrill out of killing other people. I am afraid that the events in Columbine and Aurora may trigger others bordering on psychosis to be copy-cats. Maybe Einsteins' point that the way to end wars is to eliminate armaments may also be valid in stopping senseless shootings by eliminating automatic weapons. Isn't it interesting that when James Brady who was President Reagan's press secretary took a bullet through his head that was meant for Reagan, the congress of the United States quickly passed a law restricting sale of certain weapons. That law lasted for fifteen years, but it expired and was never reinstated. This is a good example how one powerful lobby group like the National Rifle Association can influence politicians with enough money to make laws in spite of the will of the people. In fact, money corrupts even at the highest level of government.

In 1940, Gordon Allport wrote one of his classic papers known as "The Psychologist Frame of Reference," and when Einstein read it, we had a talk for several hours concerning the content. He questioned the use of the term," normal" as applied to people because he felt every individual was different and also normal. As far as he was concerned, there were no abnormal people except those suffering from psychosis, and after some vigor debate, I had to agree with what he said. However, I do believe that there are similarities among individuals especially in the way which they think that can form distinct groups and still maintain their individuality. Otherwise all the typology systems in psychology would be invalid.

After discussing all of these psychologists, Einstein favored what he called talk therapy, but only when someone was really listening to verbal and non-verbal expressions. He believed that patients should do all the talking, and therapists should do all the listening much like the approach of Carl Rogers and his indirect techniques. He told me if he ever needed counseling, he would go to a psychologist rather than a psychiatrist. During the two years that I knew him, he never consulted either one. In spite of his focus on science ideas, he really was a well rounded complete human being. The things he thoroughly enjoyed like sailing, nature walks, and playing his violin, he did with enthusiasm because they made him happy. Another source of happiness came from friends and students at Princeton. He adored young people, and always tried to encourage them to dream about their futures. I remember he had a paper on his wall from John Quincy Adams which read, "If Your Actions Inspire Others to Dream More, Learn More, Do More, and Become More, You Are a Leader." That was a perfect description of Albert Einstein. He was my mentor, and inspired me to dream more and become more, and really influenced me to live my journey through life by changing goals and direction many times. One reason I am writing this story at the ripe old age of eighty-four is that I am dreaming about the next fifteen years. He was and still is an inspiration to me and to hundreds of others who knew him.

CHAPTER VII

⌒∿⌒

EINSTEIN'S VIEWS ON THE JEWISH FAITH

Actually he did not believe that the moral attitudes of the Jewish faith were any different from all the other people. His impression was that all faiths in the modern world believed in only one higher power which some called God. While religious rituals and scriptures were very important in the beginning to get general acceptance of the moral codes of conduct, many followers have accepted the codes, but have rejected the rituals that may be in conflict with current cultural changes. As a result, the influence of Rabbis on the people has decreased soon after adolescence. He argued that rituals do not control behavior, and sermons have very little impact. It seemed to Albert that many things in the scriptures were fairy tales written by man to gain acceptance, and to make the Jews think they were the "chosen people." He opposed this idea because it had the affect of putting walls between groups of people producing negative behavior and lots of hostility. Since all people are created by God, then actually all are the chosen people. If not, how do we explain the demise of six million Jews that were killed in Hitler's concentration camps? Does a good God allow that to happen to the chosen people? The answer is of course "no". Albert believed that what did happen was God created a thinking man with a brain designed to analyze, see options, create new ideas, separate fact from fiction, solve problems even if it meant going beyond the box, and most of all to use these skills to help other human beings. To make the decisions in Germany to kill Jews was simply a man's decision. It was certainly not a Godly decision. Einstein told me that blind faith in any religion can rob its followers from the gift of choice. Some of his orthodox friends were annoyed by these thoughts and told him so. As a result he did not join a temple that I knew about. However, in spite of this, he was frequently invited and honored by many Jewish groups. I read about one such event where he proclaimed that Jewish moral principles were the foundation that all other groups could accept, and in fact were responsible for the development of social reforms around the world. It was at that event that he clarified the difference between socialistic reforms and socialism as a form of government.

So what separates the Jewish faith from other people? One thing is the sanctification of all life, not just man. He wrote, "It is characteristic that the animals were expressly included in the commands to keep holy the Sabbath day, so strong was the feeling that the ideal demands the solidarity of all living things. The insistence of the solidarity of all human beings finds still stronger expression, and it is no mere chance that the demands of Socialism were for the most part first raised by Jews." I believe he had a hidden agenda with his desire to have people stick together to cultivate an international spirit, and that agenda was to prevent the development of narrow-minded nationalism. The very moral fiber of the Jewish faith could unite us for that purpose.

The other concept he was proud of in the Jewish faith was the notion that a man's home can be his temple if he chooses. Prayer is a very personal thing, and does not have to occur in a crowd. You make a connection with your higher power when you follow basic moral principles every day. Ideas like love thy neighbor, do onto others, feed the poor, tell the truth, be loyal to your wife, and do no harm to other people were all part of Jewish tradition. If all people would live these ideals, what a wonderful world this would be. He believed, however, that accepting these moral ideals has to start with parents and children right from birth, and the best way to do this was a positive parent role model. I think Albert would have been upset when faced with the current American statistic showing three quarters of children born in our large cities have a single parent. How can these children obtain these values when the fathers have disappeared and the mothers are working day and night to make enough money to pay the bills?

The primary question for all faiths becomes how do we restore the religious moral values in our society whereby children are born into a family where both parents are there to nourish and mold them? We need a coalition of parent influence, religious influence, and societal influence to accomplish this. History teaches us that the rise and fall of all great and powerful nations has followed the demise of moral ideals.

Einstein believed that one such conflict was between the State of Israel and the Arab countries. Between 1936 and 1950, the Zionist movement in Israel produced amazingly successful work in Palestine by uniting the energy of the Jewish people. He felt strongly that it was not successful because of the British government, but was a result of a temporary partnership between the Arabs and the Jews where the needs of both were to some degree met. He did share with me that for Israel to survive in the future it needed a continued commitment to moral tradition. In his own words, "Anything we may do for the common purpose is done not merely for our brothers in Palestine, but for the well-being and honor of the whole Jewish people". He further stated in a talk to a group that. "We are assembled today for the purpose of calling to mind our age-old community, its destiny, and its problems. It is a community of moral tradition which has always shown its strength and vitality in times of stress. In all ages it had produced men who embodied the conscience of the Western world, defenders of human dignity and justice." The struggle will probably last forever, and it may take an entire generation to die off before a permanent solution is found. The wills of Jews and Arabs will be tested working through one crisis after another. What Einstein did not predict was the potential destruction of Palestine using atomic weapons by other nations like Iran. It now appears that every nation on the earth will eventually have these weapons, and may be crazy enough use them against Israel. So his earlier statement that all atomic weapons need to be destroyed seems more important today than it did sixty years ago.

Einstein's thoughts reminded me so much of the views of Wendell Willkie who ran against Franklin Roosevelt in 1940 as the Republican nominee. He was an unknown lawyer and ran as a dark horse. After he lost the election, he wrote a book that I read while in High School called "One World" where he made his famous international quote, "one world or none." Considering his views were expressed before the atomic bomb was invented, he had remarkable insight. Also, I recall that until 1939 he was a registered Democrat, converted to the Republican party, and was nominated instead of Robert Taft, Arthur Vandenberg, or Thomas Dewey. It became a battle between the isolationists and the interventionists who believed we needed to fight a war against Nazi Germany, and they believed we needed to do this for survival. Willkie was probably the first American politician that was a true internationalist. In fact his whole book was centered around the importance of all nations caring for each other. This was Einstein's view also. After the election, Dewey became a supporter of most of Roosevelt's ideas for change. He was a strong advocate for the Civil Rights movement, and so was Albert. He wanted to improve relations with China because he felt they would become a powerful force in economic matters. Since we are borrowing huge amounts of money from China, today, it seems like he was right. Einstein agreed with Willkie, but he was also projecting the same thing with the Indian nation because of their huge population. So far that has not happened. Einstein was also strongly convinced that Roosevelt's New Deal policies were very important in getting people back to work and helping to get us out of the depression. He was angry that so many politicians were labeling the New Deal effort as socialism. He wondered why feeding starving people, and getting jobs for the unemployed through the Workmans Project Administration(WPA)and the CCC camps were drawing such criticism. He pointed out to me that the vast majority of public schools, highways, bridges, and public parks were constructed through those programs. Furthermore, he felt the self respect of men when they work for government money is so much better than automatic welfare payments. What a great lesson this was, and yet here we are in 2012 still not embracing this concept. Our parks and bridges and some of our schools are falling apart. It seems like we learn nothing from events of the past. I remember he showed me a letter he wrote to one congressman about reinstating the WPA, and he received no reply. The chance of getting anything like this passed today with our two parties in gridlock is probably impossible. So we are stuck with the present welfare policy. In fact, we have extended the time to two years for welfare payments and our national debt continues to rise. I believe we now have a significant number of people in the United States who get these payments without working, and probably don't become aggressive about getting a job until the two years has ended. What has this done to their self respect?

Another person that Einstein admired was Eleanor Roosevelt, wife of the president. He liked the way she argued for the middle class in her press conferences and in her regular newspaper columns. Up to this period, president's wives were not very active. in American politics. He had a copy of one of her quotes which said something like, "We need not fear any issues in a democracy when it is achieving the ends for which it was established." That was exactly Einstein's view.

He indicated that he had corresponded with her on several occasions. He was aware that she had six children and had worked for the American Red Cross during World War two. He loved the way she spoke out for human rights, helping the poor, opposing racial discrimination, and she was very vocal about a bunch of children's issues. After the President died she became a delegate to the United Nations and appointed chair of the Human Rights Commission where she was active in writing a Universal Declaration of Human Rights which is still in existence today in the United Nations. He made it clear to me that she was a revolutionary in politics especially since she was a woman and most women were considered second class citizens in that arena.

Chapter VIII

THE FUTURE OF THE WORLD

B ased on all of our talks, I am taking a writer's privilege to speculate what Einstein would say about the future of mankind. First of all he would be quite positive about the survival of the human race. Although he recognized the threat of war as a potential world-wide demise especially with atomic weapons, he had a great deal of respect for the intelligence of man to eventually disarm everyone. He would probably say that racial issues would be resolved when an entire generation of bigots had passed, and through genetic intermarriage, all of us would be one color, I think he would speculate that all religious groups would be able to convince people around the earth to grasp and live a life based on good moral values. He would hope that the desire for material things would be replaced with the satisfaction people get when serving others, and this spirit would be contagious with all people everywhere. He would have much faith that the concept of democracy which he adored would be the model for all nations. He would envision a scientific environment that was open to new ideas, and traditional scientists would be more open-minded. He would like a change in the education of young people so that intuitive students would not be considered weird, but encouraged to use their creativity in many ways. He would hope that the motivation to become a scientist would not be limited to money, but would recognize the quest for truth as an unbelievable positive thing. He would hope that most people who fear mysterious things would learn to see this as a challenge, not a problem. He would hope that politicians put people needs above their own personal goals to get rich and be reelected. He would hope that fathers in the future would stick around and help raise their children, and that they would be better fathers than he ever was. He would hope that our leaders would learn from the mistakes made historically, and not repeat the same things that failed over and over again. He would hope that more places would grow in the world to replicate the environment of the Institute for Advanced Studies in Princeton, New Jersey. He would hope that all scientific knowledge would be translated into language that every normal citizen could understand. He would hope that all children of different personalities would be recognized as having ability to learn, and that learning style could be effective for them even if different. He would hope to see the day when social status would not be measured by monetary wealth. He would like to see the day when teachers were considered the most important people in the world. He would like to see the day when social reforms in a democracy would be perceived as a good thing because it benefits the poor as well as the rich. He would like to see Americans become internationalists and really care about all people. He would like to see men and women develop empathy and compassion that would help them to become non-judgmental towards their feelings. He would hope that young people would learn to appreciate and enjoy classical music which could add so much joy to their lives. He would hope that all kinds of prejudice in the world would be recognized that it was based on ignorance, and he especially hoped this would apply to those of the Jewish faith who had suffered so long through the years. Lastly, he would hope that you have gained something from this reading that may help you have a positive journey through your life.

CV

Stanley R. Cohen, Ed.D.
Vice-Provost
Nova Southeastern University

Earned Degrees

Bachelor of Sciences (B.S.)—1950 Rutgers University (Biology)

Masters (M.Ed.)—1955 Temple University (Administration)

Doctorate (Ed.D.)—1965 Temple University (Administration)

Professional Experience

Biology Teacher—Pleasantville High School (1952-56)

Psychological Counseling—Margate, New Jersey-Private Practice (1952-60)

Principal Woodland School, Pleasantville, New Jersey (1956-60)

Professor Glassboro State College—

Taught Courses in Education Psychology, Interaction Analysis, Supervision, Human Relations, Personality, Social Foundations (1961-1983)

Coordinator of Graduate Study in Administration (1965-81)

Behavioral Workshops—Center for the Whole Person, Philadelphia, Pennsylvania. (1971-75)

Professor and Chairman of Humanities and Behavioral Science, Professor Medical Ethics, Southeastern University, College of Osteopathic Medicine (1982-present)

Director of Instructional Development,
Southeastern University Division of the Health Sciences (1990-present)

Dean, Allied Health, Southeastern University of the Health Sciences (1992)

Vice-Provost, Nova Southeastern University of the Health Sciences (1992-present)

Professional Memberships

ADEC (Death Education)

Society of Health and Human Values

National Education Association

Phi Delta Kappa

Vice-President and President of Phi Delta Kappa (1973-74)

ABSAME (Behavioral Science in Medical Education)—Member of the Board of Directors

MERN (Michigan Ethics Resource Network)

Editorial Board for the Journal of Psychotherapy in Independent Practice

Florida Department of Corrections Ethics Network (2001)

Beacon—Quarterly—Teaching and Learning

Publications

Journal of Osteopathic Medicine, "Resident training using the MBTI," 1991

Bulletin of Research in Psychological Type (1981)

Bulletin of Research in Psychological Type (1980)

Cosiol-Jones-Cohen Children's Personality Scale (1975)

Thinking-Feeling Sensing-Intuitive Learning Patterns (1974)

Performance Based Curriculum for Urban Children (1973)

Competency Based Behavioral Objectives for Administrators (1968)

Art and Education, "Hidden Human Potential" (1965)

Jungian Personality Types—A Primer (1962)

I Am a Tree, I Can Bend—Adapting your communication style to better suit your students' needs (2006)

Peer-reviewed publications

Hardigan, P.C., Cohen, S.R., & Janoff, L.E. (2005). A comparison of personality-type among seven health professions: Implications for optometric education. *Optometric Education, 30*(2), 57-62.

Hardigan, P.C., Carvajal, M.J. & Cohen, S.R. (2000). Linking job satisfaction and career choice with personality styles: An exploratory study of practicing pharmacists. *Journal of Psychological Type, 57,* 30-35.

Hardigan, P.C. & Cohen, S.R. (1998). A comparison of osteopathic, pharmacy, physical therapy, physician assistant and occupational therapy students' personality styles: Implications for education and practice. *Journal of Pharmacy Teaching,* 32-36.

Hardigan, P.C. & Cohen, S.R. (1998). *A comparison of osteopathic, pharmacy, physical therapy, physician assistant and occupational therapy students' personality styles: Implications for education and practice.* (ERIC Document Reproduction Service No. ED 417 645).

Hardigan, P.C. & Cohen, S. R. (1998). A comparison of personality types among students enrolled in osteopathic, pharmacy, physical therapy, physician assistant and occupational programs: What the differences mean. *Journal of the American Osteopathic Society, 98,* 637-641.

Peer-reviewed abstracts

Hardigan, P.C. & Cohen, S.R. (2000). *A content analysis of questions asked of 3rd year residents during sexual education programs. Integrating Culture and Complementary Medicine: Challenges to the Biomedical Paradigm.* Association for the Behavioral Sciences and Medical Education, 29th Annual Meeting. October 12-15, 2000 / Santa Fe, NM.

Hardigan, P.C. & Cohen, S.R. (1997). *Use of the Myers-Briggs Type Indicator in medical education. Outcomes research and evaluation: The ecology of assessment in medical education*, Association for the Behavioral Sciences and Medical Education, 27th Annual Meeting, [Abstract].

Papers Presented

Hardigan, P.C. & Cohen, S.R. (July, 2004). *Creating educational tests.* American Association of Colleges of Pharmacy, Annual Meeting, Salt Lake City, UT.

Cohen, S.R. (March, 2004). *A Comprehensive Remedial Reading Program for Minority Students Grades 1-4.* Video tape presentation for teaching of reading classes at Nova Southeastern University, Ft. Lauderdale, FL.

Cohen, S.R. (October, 2003). *Using Flanders Interaction Analysis for Improvement of Classroom Instruction in the Health Professions Division of Nova Southeastern University.* Association of the Behavioral Sciences and Medical Education Annual Meeting, Charleston, SC.

Cohen, S.R. & Herzberg, G.A. (October, 2002). *Addressing Access Issues for Underserved Minority Populations Using Mezirow's Transformative Learning Experiences.* Association for Behavioral Sciences and Medical Education Annual Meeting, Lake Tahoe, CA.

Hardigan, P.C. & Cohen, S.R. (October, 1997). *Use of the Myers-Briggs Type Indicator in medical education.* Association for the Behavioral Sciences and Medical Education, Brewster, MA.

Teaching Style and Teacher Personality—
Teffrydin, Pennsylvania, 1980

Personality Profiles of Jamesburg Prisoners—
Glassboro, 1978

Predicting Teacher and Student Personality—
University of Michigan, 1977, MBTI Convention

Teaching—Learning Styles—
AACOM National Meeting, Baltimore, MD (2006)

Research

Jungian Personality Descriptions of Freshman Medical Students at Jefferson, 1970

Supervisory Ratings of Instruction in the Vineland Training School for Severly Retarded Children, 1976

Personality of Successful Athletes, 1974

A Study of the Anxiety of Children Who Cheat on Teacher-Made Tests, 1971

Development of a Kiddy Personality Scale Based on Jungian Typology, 1975 (Grant Supported)

Learning Styles in Relations to Personality Factors, 1976

Changes in Personality Factors Resulting from Academic Failure as Measured by Repeated *Rorschach* Testing of Age-Regressed College Students, Glassboro, 1965

Resolution of Discipline Problems Using Personality Data and Transactional Analysis to Resolve Conflict, Great Valley, Pennsylvania, 1981 (Grant Supported)

Comparison of Personality Styles between Students Enrolled in Osteopathic Medicine, Pharmacy, Physical Therapy, Physician Assistant, and Occupational Therapy Programs, JAOA Journal, November, 1998

SOURCES IN THE LITERATURE FOR
ALBERT EINSTEIN

Albert Einstein. (2008). Irvine, CA: Saddleback Educational Pub.

Albert Einstein. (2007). Boras: Nicotext.

Alcott, M., & Basic Skills Agency. (2000). *Albert Einstein.* London: Hodder & Stoughton.

Anand, Y. P., Einstein, A., Gandhi,., & National Gandhi Museum (New Delhi, India). (2006). *Albert Einstein and Mahatma Gandhi: The cent or, o Avsics, war, satvagraha, and peace.* New Delhi: National Gandhi Museum.

Barnes, T. H., Royal Society of New Zealand., & National Radio (N.Z.). (2006). *The e egant universe a 'Albert Einstein: The collected lectures of the Royal Society of New Zealand E-r-inc2 series, broadcast on National Radio.* Wellington, N.Z: Awa Press.

Belanger, C., & EBSCO Publishing (Firm). (2006). *Albert Einstein.* *S.1.:* Great Neck Pub. Bjerknes, C. J. (2002). *Albert Einstein:*

The incorrigible plagiarist. Downers Grove, Ill: XTX. Boehm, G. (2005). Pf'ho *was Albert Einstein?.* New York: Assouline.

Brockman, J. (2004). *curious minds': 'wenty-seven scientists escribe what inspired them to choose theirTaths.* New York: Pantheon Books.

Brockman, J. (2006). M.:1,,,./,:i4p,,s1:01;_,Ay_i..-ty,y i?j; tweniy-finv *of the world's leading thinkers' on the man, his work; and his legacy.* New York: Pantheon Books.

Calaprice, A., & Lipscombe, T. (2005). *Albert Einstein.* Westport, Conn: Greenwood Press.

Carl Rogers.(1946). Some Observations on the Organization of Personality. Psychological Review. 2.APA

Clark Hull.(1937). Mind, Mechanism, and Adaptive Behavior. Psychological Review.44.APA

Cohen, Stan, (2005) I Am a Tree, I Can Bend, Publish America, Baltimore, Md.

Edward L. Thorndike.(1913). Ideo Motor Action. Psychological Review, 20, APA.

Edward Tolman.(1938). The Determiners of Behavior at a Choice Point, Psychological Review.44.APA

Einstein, A., Kormos, **B. D.,** *& Sauer, T. (2009). <u>The collected papers of Albert Einstein: Volume</u> 12. Princeton (N.J.: Princeton University Press.*

Einstein, A., Engel, A.., & Schucking, E. (2002). *The collected papers ojAl er.Einstein: En_glish translation or selected texts.* Princeton, N.J: Princeton University Press.

Einstein, A., & Hawking, S. W. (2007). A stubbornLpersistent illusion: The essential scientYie writin 241bert <u>Einstein.</u> Philadelphia: Running Press.

Einstein, A., Born, H., Born, M., **Born,** *I., & Born, G. (2005). <u>The Born-Einstein letters:</u> Friendship, politics andphysics in uncertain limes : corre,sponde 11C e between Albert Einstein und Max and Iledwig Born from 1916 to 1955. New York: Macmillan.*

Einstein, A., Kormos, **B. D.,** *& Sauer, T. (2009). The collected papers oillbert ':instein: Volume <u>12.</u> Princeton (N.J.: Princeton University Press.*

Einstein, A., Born, M., & Born, H. (2005). <u>The Born-Einstein letters:</u> <u>Friendship, politics, and physics in uncertain times : correspondence</u>

between Albert Einstein and Max and [iedwjg Born from 19.16 to 1955 with commentaries by Itax Born. Houndmills, Basingstoke, Hampshire: Macmillan.

Einstein, A. (2000). *Albert—Einstein in his own words in two complete books: Relativity-the J'..mcial and—^{Y}e ner al theory: Out o later years-the scientist) hilos(»her and man portrayed through his own words'.* New York: Portland House.

Einstein, A., & Swisher, C. (2001). *Albert Einstein.* San Diego: Greenhaven Press.

Einstein, A., & Klein, M. J. (2003). *Einstein's 1912 manuscript on the special theory (?I' relativity.* New York: George Braziller, in association with the Edmond J. Safra Philanthropic Foundation.

Einstein, A., & Calaprice, A. (2002). *Dear Professor Einstein: Albert instein's letters to and from children.* Amherst, N.Y: Prometheus Books.

Einstein, A., & Swisher, C. (2001). *Albert Einstein.* San Diego: Greenhaven Press.

Einstein-Mario, M., & Popovie, M. (2003). *In Albert's shadow: The lije and letters o Marie, Einstein's first tvik.* Baltimore: Johns Hopkins University Press.

Garbedian, H. G. (2000). *Albert Einstein: Maker of universes.* Whitefish, Mont: Kessinger,

Ghatak, A. K. (2011). *Albert Einstein,' gliniip_se of his life,_philosoph* and science. New Delhi: Viva Books.

Gordon Allport.(1940). The Psychologist's Frame of Reference. Psychological Review.37.APA Green, J. (2003). <u>*Albert Einstein.*</u> Melbourne, Vic: Ocean Press.

Greene, R., Brizel, F., Robbins, A., Thomas, H., & Greenfield, J. (2002). <u>*Words that shook*</u> the *}yorfd. New York: Prentice Hall.*

Gribbin, J. R., & Gribbin, M. (2005). *Annus mirabilis: 1905* <u>*Albert*</u> *Einstein, am lie theory of* <u>*relativity.*</u> *New York: Chamberlain Bros.*

Gribbin, J. R., & Gribbin. M. (2005). <u>*Annii iii.ᵗahilis: 190i Albert Li*</u> <u>*relativity.*</u> *New York: Chamberlain Bros.*

Hall, D., & Hall, S. G. (2006). American *iC01·1,S" An encʸclopedia* <u>*of*</u> the people, yloces, and <u>*things that have shaped our culture.*</u> Westport, Conn: Greenwood Press.

Hentschel, A., Grasshoff, G., & Graff, K. W. (2005). <u>*Albert Einstein:*</u> <u>*"Those happy Bertlese*</u> Bern: Stdmpfli.

Henry Marshall.(1908). The Methods of the Naturalist and Psychologist. Psychological Review,15,APA

Illy, J. (2006). *Albert meets America: How journalists treated gV11111-S during Einstein's 1921, travel.* Baltimore, Md: Johns Hopkins University Press.

Janssen, M., Besso, M., & Janssen, M. (2003). Albert Einstein, 187 1955. Paris (120 Av. des Champstlysees, 75008: Scriptura-Aristophil.

John Dewey.(1900) Psychology and Social Practice, Psychological Review. APA Kaku, M. (2004). *Einstein's cosmos: flaw Albert Einstein's vision int.,lbrined our undertp.idipgpt space and time.* London: Weidenfeld & Nicolson.

Keeble, T. (2003). Albert Einstein. Melbourne: Ocean.

Kesselring, S. (2010). 4.1bert *Einstein.* Mankato, Minn: The child's world.

Knight Dunlap.(1923). The Foundation of Social Psychology. Psychological Review, 30.APA Krstie, D. (2003).11/illeva *.C'e: Albert Ein,sfein: .Love and joint „svienti 'vork.* S.1: s.n..

Krstie, D. (2004). *Mileva & Albert Einstein: Their love and scientific collaboration.* Radovljica, Slovenia: Didakta.

Lacayo, R. (2011). Einstein: *The enduring egaty of a modern genius.* New York: Time Books. Lacayo, R. (2011). *Albert Einstein.* New York: Time Home Entertainment.

Lamb, B. (2004). *Booknotes: On American chart:10er.* New York: PublicAffairs.

Marie, M., Popovie, M., & Marie, M. (2003). *In Albert's shadow: The life and letters of Mileva Marit:', Einstein's first wife.* Baltimore, Md. [etc.: The Johns Hopkins University Press.

Mih, W. C. (2000). *The ji.tsvinating lit ant theory fAlbert Einstein.* Huntington, N.Y: Kroshka Books.

Mik-WTe:-(2000). *Thejascinatinl iuii iyolAtbert Einstein.* Huntington, N. Y: KroshkaBooks.

Mishra, V. K. (2008). *Albert Einstein: The life of a genius.* New Delhi, India: Ocean Books. Murthi, R. K. (2006). *Albert Einstein: A short biography.* New Delhi: Rupa & Co.

Pais, A., & Penrose, R. (2005). *"Subtle is the L rd.": The science and the lift? (?t]ilbeir Einstein.* Oxford: Oxford University Press.

Pasachoff, N. E., & World Book, Inc. (2007). *Albert Einstein: With) rofiles*

Pickering, F., & Davis, M. (2006).—Beijing: Foreign Language Teaching and Research Press.

Renn, J., & Max-Planck-Institut ffir Wissenschaftsgeschichte. (2005) *AIheiiEinstciuchief engineer of the universe.* Weinheim: Wiley-VCH-Verlag.

Renn, J. (2005). *Albert Einslein—chiet engineer of /he universe: One hundred au/hors fbi Einstein.* Weinheim: Wiley-VCH.

Renn, J. (2005). *Albert Einslein—!hi context.* Weinheim: Wiley-VCH.

Renn, J., & Max-Planck-Institut fur Wissenschaftsgeschichte. (2005). *Albert des I :niversums Dokumente eines LebensI•e^{Y}es.* Berlin: Wiley-VHC.

Robert Yerkes.(1918). Psychology in Relation to War. Psychological Review.25.APA

Robinson, A., & Bet ha-sefarim ha-leHumi yeha-universitaEi bi-Yerushalayim. (2005). *zI hulk Iva 'years qJ i clativij.* New York: Harry N. Abrams.

Rosenkranz, Z., Wolff, B., Rosenkranz, Z., Bet ha-sefarim ha-le Humi yeha-universitaDi biYerushalayim., Bet ha-sefarim ha-le Liumi yeha-universitaEi bi-Yerushalayim., & Universitah ha-1`1Ivrit bi-Yerushalayim. (2007). illbcrI *I ilislein 11e persisieni illusion of transience.* Israel: Magnes Press.

Saddleback Educational Publishing. (2008). *Albeit Einstein.* Irvine: Saddleback Educational Pub, Schilpp, P. A. (2000). *Albert Einstein: Philosopher-set-enlist.* New York: MFJ Books.

Shmoop University Inc. (2010)..4lbert *Einstein.* Sunnyvale, Calif.: Shmoop University.

Silvers, R. B., & Epstein, B. (2009). *The company,' cy kept: Writers on unfOrgenable friendships.* New York: New York Review.

Simone, P. G. (2008). <u>*Were Albert Einstein and Charles Darwin idiots?: A brief lesson in*</u> environmental science. Victoria, BC: Trafford.

Srinivasan, A. (2006). *Nobel laureates.* Chennai: Sura Books.

Stefan, V. A. (2006). *Albert and Mileva Einstein, World Year of Physics 2005, and more.* La Jolla, CA: Stefan University Press.Steiner, F. (2007). <u>*Albert Einstein: On the occasion 25th anniversary of his birth in U*</u> Berlin: Springer.Stern, F. R. (2001).

United States. (2004). *Federal Bureau of Investigation 1Freedom ofinjormation Actj: Subject /f^{les}/* Washington, DC: Federal Bureau of Investigation.

Stanley R. Cohen, Ed.D.

William James.(1894). The Knowing of Things Together, Psychological
Review 2, APA

Whitfield, D., & Hicks, J. L. (2007). *What's the matter?: Readings in physics.* Chicago, IL: Great Books Foundation.